vegan express

Vegan
express

Written and illustrated by
Nava Atlas

BROADWAY BOOKS   NEW YORK

PUBLISHED BY BROADWAY BOOKS

Published in the United States by Broadway Books,
an imprint of The Doubleday Broadway Publishing Group,
a division of Random House, Inc., New York.
www.broadwaybooks.com

BROADWAY BOOKS and its logo, a letter B bisected on the diagonal,
are trademarks of Random House, Inc.

Library of Congress Cataloging-in-Publication Data
Atlas, Nava.
      Vegan express/ written and illustrated by Nava Atlas. — 1st ed.
        p.   cm.
      Includes index.
      1. Vegan cookery. I. Title.

   TX837.A8472 2008
   641.5'636—dc22
   2007034881

ISBN 978-0-7679-2617-1

PRINTED IN THE UNITED STATES OF AMERICA

10   9   8   7   6   5   4   3   2   1

First Edition

contents

foreword

As you page through the recipes in this book, you will find flavors from one end of the world to the other, and your mouth will water with every turn of the page. But not only will your taste buds thank you. Your body will thank you, too.

Fueling your body with plant-based foods can revolutionize your health—perhaps even save your life. By setting aside meat, fish, dairy, and eggs, and bringing in healthful whole foods, you open the door to remarkable results. A vegan diet is healthful for everyone and *Vegan Express* makes it simpler than ever to enjoy delicious and healthy food in no time at all.

So many people have made wrong turns in their search for the perfect diet. A switch from red meat to white meat, for example, really does not do the job. You might scrupulously limit meat intake to no more than six ounces per day, favor chicken and fish while trimming away visible fat, and choose skim over whole milk and egg whites over whole eggs, but you would find the results to be embarrassingly modest. Cholesterol levels fall by only about five percent. Body weight and blood pressure improve only modestly. Inside the arteries, blockages continue to worsen. All in all, there is little reward for all this effort. Americans now eat, believe it or not, one million chickens per hour, and collectively we are more out of shape than at any time in our nation's history.

Numerous scientific studies have shown that the healthiest diet of all is one that is low in fat and is completely comprised of plant foods. Vegetarians have healthier hearts, healthier skin, lower blood pressure, less risk of diabetes, fewer kidney stones and gallstones, and forty percent less cancer risk. Part of the reason, of course, is that vegetarian diets are naturally lower in fat and cholesterol, and higher in fiber than non-vegetarian diets. Vegan diets are best of all, since they are essentially cholesterol-free (our bodies make all the cholesterol they need), and contain zero animal fat or animal protein. Also, vegetarians are, on average, ten percent slimmer than non-vegetarians. A diet based on whole grains, legumes, vegetables, and fruit is low in calories and fat and rich in fiber to satisfy your appetite. Get ready to feel great.

If you are tempted to put it to the test, I suggest that you take a week or two and try out as many of these delicious recipes as you can. Then, when you have found your favorites, block out a three-week period to eat low-fat, vegan foods exclusively. Don't just put your toe in the swimming pool; go ahead and dive in. As you get started, your body will begin to transform itself. In all likelihood, you'll start to lose weight, your cholesterol will fall, your energy level will improve, and you'll feel better than you've felt since you were a kid. If after three weeks, you like the feeling of a healthier, trimmer body, you can stick with it. In *Vegan Express,* Nava gives you all the tools you need to put this powerful diet to work in the most delicious way possible.

Best in health,
Neal Barnard, MD
President, Physicians Committee for Responsible Medicine
(pcrm.org)

acknowledgments

Many thanks to the talented people who contributed in significant ways to this book:

Susan Voisin (fatfreevegan.com and sbvdesigns.com) created the lovely photos in the insert of this book. Susan, I didn't know my recipes could look so good.

Nikki Goldbeck, CDN (healthyhighways.com), did the nutritional analyses of the recipes. It was wonderful to have one of the true pioneers of vegetarian food and nutrition writing involved in this book.

Neal Barnard, MD, who wrote the foreword to this book, is such an eminent authority on vegan diets and such an energetic promoter of the vegan way of life that I'm truly honored by his contribution.

This is my third book with Broadway Books, and I'm as impressed as ever with their attention to detail and their care at every stage of a book's production. Special thanks go to Kristen Green and Elizabeth Rendfleisch. I always save the last thanks for my wonderful editor, Jennifer Josephy; this time, though, I'll add "happy anniversary" to these thanks. This book is being published in 2008, exactly 20 years from the time Jennifer first became my editor. For this rare gift of endurance in the publishing world, I'm especially grateful!

vegan express

Introduction

Coming home from camp one day several years ago, my younger son (then only ten years old) announced: "Now I'm a vegan." Since Evan had been a lifelong vegetarian (like his older brother, Adam) and is the child of committed vegetarian parents, this wasn't as much of a shock as when, decades ago, I informed my meat-eating family that I was becoming a vegetarian. Still, when I emptied his lunch box and saw that he had left his rice cheese sandwich uneaten (mistaking it for dairy cheese), my Typical Mom reaction was, "Couldn't you have become a vegan after lunch?"

I had been privately considering going vegan, so when my older son promptly followed his younger brother's lead, I decided to take the plunge as well. My husband took a short while longer to give up eggs, but soon we were all back on the same page—or more accurately, the same plate. Ours was a fairly typical transition—longtime lacto-ovo vegetarians gradually giving up eggs and dairy, then taking the final leap from vegetarian to vegan. We've never looked back.

Most of the people reading this book will already have a clear picture of what it means to be a vegan. If this applies to you, feel free to skim or skip this paragraph. For anyone who needs a crash course, here goes: Vegetarians avoid meat, fowl, and seafood; vegans avoid all animal products in the diet (including eggs, dairy products, and honey) as well as in their lifestyle. For most vegans, ethical factors are equally as important as health and environmental issues. Concerns for animal welfare and the embracing of a more compassionate lifestyle mean that full-fledged vegans won't eat honey or wear leather; in general, any products that are derived from animals or that contain animal by-products are avoided. Vegans also scrupulously avoid products known to have been tested on animals.

And no, vegans are not necessarily young, hip, and tattooed, as the media might have you think, though that's not to say that there aren't a fair number who might fit that description. However, vegans are, by and large, extremely cool, even if they are no longer young!

It has become much easier to be vegan out in the wider world—perhaps not in the hinterlands, but certainly in every decent-sized city I've visited at home and abroad. In addition, nearly every semienlightened locale, urban or exurban, has loads of great places to eat and shop for food. International restaurants abound with healthy meatless choices. My family members rarely, if ever, feel frustrated or restricted. When we need to let people know that we're vegans, whether in restaurants or at gatherings, we often receive looks of admiration rather than confusion (or contempt!). What a change from twenty-five or thirty years ago, when merely being a vegetarian branded you as some sort of weirdo.

My family lives a couple hours north of New York City. Here we don't even have a Whole Foods market, and Trader Joe's is just far enough away that it's out of our shopping range. We do have some decent natural foods stores, as well as the Hannaford's supermarket chain. This store is starting to bear a striking resemblance to Whole Foods (except that the prices at the former are more reasonable), as natural products, organic produce, and ethnic foods become everyday items. From what I've seen during my travels, it seems this trend is spreading. Supermarkets are responding to consumer demand for more natural foods, making it easy to obtain products and produce not long ago deemed esoteric. So, if I can fulfill our family's vegan food needs where I live, chances are you can, too; and if you can't today, you'll likely be able to very soon, as the American supermarket is changing rapidly.

To supplement our grocery shopping during warmer months, much of our produce comes from the local community-supported agriculture (CSA) farm to which we belong, as well as from

farmers' markets. See if there's one you can join near where you live. It's easy to make incredible-tasting meals when the basic ingredients are so fresh and flavorful.

Before going vegan, I worried that family meals might be impossibly restrictive, but making the transition was surprisingly easy. With the variety of nondairy cheeses and milks so readily available, we can still enjoy favorite cheesy and creamy dishes. And as I discovered in creating my previous book, *The Vegetarian Family Cookbook,* eggs are entirely unnecessary for creating tender, delectable baked goods. However, being vegan is not just about substituting one kind of cheese for another so that you can still have pizza. The optimal vegan diet, like any ideal diet, is abundant with fresh organic fruits and vegetables, including plenty of leafy greens, whole grains, beans and other legumes, nuts and seeds, and soy products. Even if you have no intention of going vegan full time, anyone can enjoy (and benefit from) completely plant-based meals on a regular basis.

A WORD ABOUT THE RECIPES AND MENUS

I wrote this book at a particularly busy time in my life. I won't bore you with the details except the most significant, which is that while writing it, I was also in graduate school (having returned after a twenty-seven-year gap in my education), working on a thesis in art studio. In retrospect, this was not the wisest of combinations—please, don't even think about writing a book and working on a thesis at the same time—unless, of course, the book is your thesis! Which, in my case, it was not.

The fact that I survived this stretch of time, producing both a vegan cookbook and a thesis, with teenagers still at home, was living proof of one thing: These recipes really do fit into a busy (perhaps overly busy) life. Most of the individual recipes in this book can be made in thirty minutes or less, and the majority have enough downtime in their preparation process during which to make a simple accompaniment—a salad or vegetable side dish, or a complementary companion dish. Only occasionally will a recipe take more than thirty minutes, mainly for cooking brown rice or roasting vegetables; but in these cases, I strive to ensure that hands-on time is kept to a minimum.

Chapters Two through Six contain recipes around which meals can be built as well as menu suggestions. There are ideas on how to complete each meal, often with other recipes from this book, as well as tips for completing meals without using further recipes. With these recipes, menus, and recipe-free ideas, you can build a scrumptious meal, often in thirty to forty-five minutes total. None of the suggestions are etched in stone; the format of this book allows you to mix and match as you like. Once you've developed a repertoire of favorite recipes, it will be easy and fun for you to create combinations beyond those suggested here.

In addition, you'll find tips in many of the chapters on preparing tofu, pastas, grain dishes, salads, wraps, vegetable side dishes, and more, without formal recipes. Certain dishes benefit more from inspiration than from precise measurements. Take wraps, for example. You might appreciate a slew of ideas that tap into ingredients you have on hand more than exact measures of how much of each to put in the wrap. Maybe you want to make only one wrap for a brown-bag lunch or a solo dinner. Or perhaps you'd like to arrange some tasty fillings on the table and let diners make their own wraps, just the way they like them. Similarly, in salads based on mixed greens, exact amounts of additional ingredients matter less than creative combinations.

VEGAN NUTRITION BASICS

I imagine that most readers of this book are already familiar and comfortable with the vegan diet and lifestyle. But for those just starting to explore an entirely plant-based diet, or for those who wish to share information about such a plan with skeptical family members or friends, here are a few basics.

Brenda Davis, RD, and Vesanto Melina, MS, RD, authors of

Becoming Vegan, state: "The vast majority of studies assessing the dietary intakes and nutritional status of vegans reassure us that well-planned vegan diets can supply adequate nutrition . . . It is important to recognize, however, that as with nonvegetarian or lacto-ovo vegetarian diets, vegan diets can be both adequate and inadequate." *Becoming Vegan* is quite possibly the best resource in print for learning about and transitioning to a vegan diet, if you'd like detailed information. A great Web resource is the Vegetarian Resource Group's site (vrg.org). There you will find a wealth of vegan nuts and bolts, including articles on nutritional needs from infancy to adulthood. Request their brochure, "Vegan Diets in a Nutshell," which suggests ways to obtain protein, calcium, zinc, iron, and vitamins D and B12. Becoming a member of VRG entitles you to *Vegetarian Journal,* a quarterly publication of vegan nutrition, ethics, and recipes. Though there is no shortage of sound information on vegan diets both in print and on the Web, these two are excellent sources if you are just starting out.

A plant-based diet is considered by many experts to be ideal. *The China Study,* led by Dr. T. Colin Campbell (and detailed in a best-selling book of the same name) is considered the largest study of human nutrition ever done. Dr. Campbell came to the conclusion that "People who ate the most animal-based foods got the most chronic disease . . . People who ate the most plant-based foods were the healthiest and tended to avoid chronic disease." Though there seems to be an occasional, yet persistent backlash against veganism, arguments for a well-planned plant-based diet are, when the evidence is presented, difficult to refute.

In a diet rich in whole grains, legumes, vegetables, and fruits, one is almost assured of getting an optimal amount of a broad range of vitamins and minerals. A plant-based diet is almost by definition high in fiber, another great benefit. And it's not

difficult to get your daily dose of valuable omega-3 fatty acids with 1 to 2 teaspoons of flaxseed or hempseed oil, or a handful of walnuts or hemp nuts. The main areas in which questions on vegan diets arise are protein, calcium, vitamin D, and vitamin B12, so we'll tackle those individually.

PROTEIN: The body can manufacture all but nine of the 22 amino acids that make up proteins. These nine amino acids are referred to as indispensable (formerly known as "essential") amino acids and must be derived from food. That's why getting sufficient, good quality protein is crucial. And sufficient is the operative concept here: Excess protein can't be stored, and its elimination puts a strain on internal organs. The World Health Organization's "Technical Report 797" states: "There are no known advantages from increasing the proportion of energy derived from protein (15% of total calories) and high intakes may have harmful effects in promoting excessive losses of body calcium and perhaps in accelerating age-related decline in renal (kidney) function."

Here is how to calculate how much protein you need. The Recommended Daily Allowance (RDA), established by the National Academy of Sciences, states that an adult in good health needs 0.36 grams of protein per pound of body weight. Thus, a 160-pound man needs about 58 grams of protein a day, and a 120-pound woman needs about 43 grams.

Exceptions to the RDA guidlines are as follows: Pregnant and lactating women need considerably more protein—add at least 25 grams of protein per day. Infants and children need more total protein per body pound than adults. For toddlers age one through three years, calculate 0.5 grams per pound of body weight; children four through 13 years, 0.43 grams per pound, and teens, 0.39 grams per pound.

A persistent myth is that vegan diets do not provide adequate protein. Nutritional wisdom dictates, however, that if the diet is varied and provides sufficient calories, there is very little chance that protein supply could be inadequate. Protein is not hard to get in a vegan diet, since all foods, with the exception of sugars and oils, have at least some protein. Whole grains, legumes, soy products, and nuts and seeds, which are the building blocks of a healthy vegan diet, are superb sources of protein. Many vegetables have notable amounts of protein, so if you eat plenty of them, those add up as well.

CALCIUM: Media advertising has helped our national conscious-ness conflate calcium with dairy products. However, in some circles, there is doubt over whether dairy products offer the best source of absorbable calcium; indeed, many studies have shown that in countries with the highest use of dairy have the highest incidence of osteoporosis as well. It is postulated that animal protein may leach calcium from the bones.

Calcium is known for its role in the formation and maintenance of bones and teeth. It also assists in muscle contraction, blood clotting, and nerve function. Some good vegan sources are tofu (especially if prepared with calcium sulfate), quinoa, sesame seeds, almonds, dark green leafy vegetables (especially kale, collards, and spinach), fortified foods like soymilk and orange juice, dried figs, many sea vegetables, and blackstrap molasses.

VITAMIN B12: This nutrient is essential for general growth and for the functions of the blood cells and nervous system. Apart from tempeh and some sea vegetables (which are not considered reliable sources) B12 is not found in plant sources, and so vegans are advised to make sure to use fortified soymilk, fortified meat analogs, fortified breakfast cereals, or vegetarian vitamin supplements. Red Star Vegetarian Support Formula nutritional yeast is an additional source. Only a very small amount of B12 is needed for good health. It is important to get it, but not at all difficult.

VITAMIN D: Our bodies need vitamin D in order to absorb calcium and phosphorus, which are crucial to the formation and maintenance of bones and teeth. We've come to associate vitamin D with milk, though it is not a component of dairy; rather, milk is supplemented with it, as is soymilk as well as enriched rice milk. Many experts agree, though, that the best and most absorbable form of vitamin D comes from brief (10 to 15 minutes) daily exposure to sunlight. If your diet is in short supply of vitamin D foods or sunlight exposure, make sure to supplement. Vitamin D is contained in many standard vitamin supplements.

When you strive to create an entire meal in thirty to forty-five minutes, shortcuts are a necessity. Using natural, convenient products like salsa, peanut satay sauce, salad dressings, flavored varieties of tofu, and canned beans and lentils give you the time and leisure to include lots of produce (which almost invariably needs a certain amount of prep time). Even if time is short, I like to prepare dishes that abound with fresh ingredients. That's not to say I never make sauces, dressings, and the like from scratch. I do, and you'll find evidence of that in these pages. The point is that the availability of high-quality prepared natural products allows you to strike a balance between freshness and convenience when time is an issue.

It hardly needs to be said that keeping your pantry and refrigerator stocked with a good assortment of ingredients goes a long way to reducing the "what should I make for dinner?" dilemma. And as I've long advocated, plan two or three meals before each shopping trip. It will save you lots of time in the long run, I promise! Here's a basic pantry list tailored to the meals in this book.

PRODUCTS I LOVE FOR *VEGAN EXPRESS* MEALS

Explanation of Nutritional Analyses

• All breakdowns are based on 1 serving. When a recipe gives a range in the number of servings—for example, 4 to 6 servings—the analysis is based on the average number of servings; in this case, 5 servings.

• When more than one ingredient is listed as an option, the first ingredient is used in the analysis. Usually, the optional ingredient will not change the analysis significantly.

• Ingredients listed as optional (e.g., "chopped cashews, optional") are not included in the analysis.

• When salt is listed "to taste," its sodium content is not included in the analysis.

• These analyses were done by someone with skill and expertise, but please note that they are "best estimates." Especially when using prepared products like tortillas, salsa, beans, and such, analyses will vary depending on the brand used. These were done with my preferred brands; using yours, the statistics may vary—not wildly, but they will vary nonetheless.

• And finally, you will note that the recipes have not been analyzed for cholesterol, which is usually included in standard analyses. This is because plant foods contain no cholesterol. So, to avoid a great deal of redundancy, note that the cholesterol content in all recipes is zero.

Produce

Keeping an array of fresh produce in the refrigerator year-round goes a long way toward guaranteeing healthy, delicious meals on a regular basis. The availability of fruits and vegetables once restricted to a specific season has widened dramatically; still, I prefer to use produce that reflects seasonal availability as much as possible. It tastes better, as it's more likely to have ripened naturally than "fresh" fruits and veggies that were developed to withstand a long time in transit. Who wants winter squash in July or strawberries in January? This kind of eating seems counter-intuitive; it's not as much fun, either. It does away with pleasures like savoring fresh-picked strawberries in May or June, or anticipating the arrival of spring when the first bundles of asparagus appear in the market. When those strawberries and asparagus are on the shelves in November, it's hard to know which season is which any longer, at least in terms of produce (climate change is not helping the situation, either). Here's a basic list of what to keep on hand:

IN THE PANTRY: Potatoes (and sweet potatoes in fall, winter, and early spring), onions, garlic

IN THE VEGETABLE DRAWER: Broccoli, cauliflower, celery, red and/or green cabbage, carrots and/or baby carrots, zucchini, lettuce, bell peppers, cucumbers, scallions

IN THE FRUIT DRAWER: Apples, pears, oranges, lemons, limes

ON THE COUNTER: Tomatoes, cherry and/or grape tomatoes, bananas

You'll want to pick up some produce when it is in season:

SEASONAL AND OCCASIONAL PRODUCE: Swiss chard, kale, asparagus, daikon radish, turnips, beets, leeks, Brussels sprouts, green beans, eggplant, yellow summer squash, corn on the cob, avocados, berries, melons, stone fruits

Finally, here are three fresh ingredients that, not so long ago, were hard to find. Now they're in nearly every supermarket, and I use them regularly.

MIXED BABY GREENS: This is one salad staple I just can't do without. With these colorful greens, all you need is a handful of other ingredients (other vegetables as well as fruits, nuts, mushrooms, and so on) to create an appetizing salad. Explore some fun possibilities under Recipe Not Required To Make Dazzling Green Salads (page 192).

BABY SPINACH: Not so long ago, the thought of dealing with a big bundle of muddy, long-stemmed spinach leaves when I was in a hurry would send me straight to the freezer for frozen chopped spinach (a product that leaves much to be desired). Now, the constant availability of organic baby spinach has changed this. All it needs is a quick rinse and a minute of exposure to heat (unless being used raw in salads). Baby spinach has made frozen spinach a thing of the past for me; it adds wonderful color and flavor to many kinds of dishes.

FINGERLING POTATOES: These diminutive potatoes have a long, narrow shape—hence their name. They come in several varieties; I like to use organic golden fingerlings like Russian Banana. For added drama, there's a purple-fleshed variety from Peru. They often come in $1\frac{1}{2}$-pound bags, though you can sometimes buy them in bulk. Their tiny, narrow shape allows them to cook quickly. My favorite way to prepare fingerlings is to make quick, fresh fries (see recipe on page 194).

Canned, Jarred, and Packaged Products

BEANS: Always keep a variety of canned beans, a top pantry staple, on hand. The ones used most in this book are black beans, chickpeas, pink or red beans, and cannellini. Note that organic canned beans are packed with far less sodium than standard brands. In either case, draining and rinsing is recommended to wash away some of the salt.

NATURAL, SALT-FREE BOUILLON CUBES: Bouillon cubes are useful for making quick soups as well as for infusing the cooking water for grains with extra flavor. Make sure to choose an all-natural brand, preferably one with no trans fats or salt (after all, it's the concentration of herbs and spices we're after, not extra sodium). My favorite brand is Rapunzel.

COCONUT MILK: A few years ago, this would have been a once-in-a-while item in my kitchen, but now I always keep a few cans on hand for making delicious Thai-style soups, noodle dishes, stews, and sauces. I prefer light coconut milk, which contains less fat than the whole-fat variety.

LENTILS: Canned lentils have become more common these last few years as cooks have gotten ever more time-crunched. When you want to put dinner on the table quickly, even the relatively fast cooking time of lentils can be a bit much. Organic canned brown lentils taste good and hold their shape nicely. And if you ever come across canned beluga lentils (a tiny black variety), give them a try. They don't taste all that different, but their attractive appearance gives dishes a little more flair.

NONHYDROGENATED MARGARINE: I use margarine occasionally and sparingly, where a buttery flavor is desired. When I use margarine, I prefer the natural brand Earth Balance, which is trans-fat free and low in saturated fat. The supermarket equivalent of Earth Balance is Smart Balance; both are made by the same company, and from what I can tell, are very similar products.

RICE MILK: I'm not a big fan of cooking with soymilk (such as in soups, sauces, or other creamy dishes). Its beany, slightly sweet taste comes through in a way that I find off-putting. I much prefer the more neutral flavor of rice milk. Rice Dream Original Enriched is the brand I use most often. It comes in 32-ounce aseptic cartons that keep for a long time in the pantry.

SILK CREAMER: I occasionally call for this soy-based cream substitute in small amounts where a dense, creamy consistency is desired. Use the plain-flavored original, of course.

SUN-DRIED TOMATOES: A few oil-packed sun-dried tomatoes go a long way to create bursts of flavor in all kinds of dishes. For greater convenience, you can purchase dried tomatoes that are already cut into strips.

VEGAN CHEESES: In the recipes, I call for "vegan cheese" rather than "soy cheese" That's so readers can opt to use rice- or almond-based cheeses, as well as the more common soy cheese. Savvy vegans are well aware that many of these alternative cheeses contain a minute amount of casein, a milk protein that helps the cheeses melt. Some vegans are comfortable with that, while others are not. My favorite brand is Vegan Gourmet, a meltable soy-based cheese made without casein. It comes in mozzarella, Monterey Jack, cheddar, and nacho flavors. By the time this book sees print, it's possible that there will be other casein-free brands on the market.

VEGETABLE STOCK: For brothy and Asian soups, I like to keep a couple of 32-ounce aseptic cartons of stock in the pantry. When you want to make a soup that will be ready in thirty minutes or less, these lend a needed head start for creating flavor. Look for an all-natural ingredient list, with lots of herbs and seasonings and less sodium.

PLUS A FEW ONCE-IN-A-WHILE ITEMS: For fun and variety, the recipes in this book use marinated artichoke hearts, roasted red peppers, cured black olives, and green pimiento-stuffed olives. Whether you'd like to stock them as staples depends on the size of your pantry. If there's room, keep them on hand; if not, buy as needed.

Pasta and Noodles

Keep a good supply on hand for making Asian-style, Italian, and fusion pasta dishes. For the former, that would include soba (buckwheat noodles), udon, and bean thread (cellophane) noodles; for a change of pace, try rice vermicelli as well.

For other kinds of pasta dishes, a small assortment of short, chunky shapes (cavatappi, gemelli, penne, farfalle—whatever you prefer) is good to have in the pantry. Long, thin pastas like angel hair or spaghettini come in handy as well.

Frozen Vegetables

I'm actually not a huge fan of frozen veggies, with a few exceptions. I always keep peas and corn in the freezer, as they are both useful and relatively tasty. And since the window for really good, fresh green beans is so limited, I occasionally buy whole baby green beans, which are actually pretty decent. A good once-in-a-while frozen item is shelled edamame (fresh green soybeans). As with fresh produce, I prefer organic frozen vegetables.

Condiments

Aside from the basics, like ketchup, mustard, and vegan mayonnaise, here are the products I find most useful to keep on hand.

AGAVE NECTAR: The vegan answer to honey, this natural sweetener is derived from a type of cactus. Fluid and golden like honey, supersweet but not assertive, a little goes a long way. Agave is kind to the system, with a low glycemic index, which means that it doesn't shock blood sugar levels as do simple sugars.

GINGER: You know how some people just can't live without garlic? Well, I'm not one of them. I like it fine if used in moderation, but give me ginger any time. The trouble with fresh ginger is that you never know what you're going to get—will it be fresh and moist inside, or dry and stringy? To avoid unpleasant surprises, I keep a jar or two each of minced and grated ginger on hand. My favorite brand is Ginger People, though there are other brands to choose from. Jarred ginger is always moist and fresh tasting, and a nice little time-saver when making quick meals.

LEMON AND LIME JUICE: Stock fresh lemons and limes, by all means, but for those times when you happen to be out of one or the other, it's handy to keep one bottle each of lemon and lime juice in the fridge; and in truth, they can be a handy shortcut. Splash on salads and cooked veggies, use them in dressings and sauces—citrus is great for the digestive system and reduces the need for salt.

MARINARA SAUCE: So many varieties, so many flavors; choose whatever kind you like with ingredients that please your palate— herbs, garlic, wine, mushrooms, chunky vegetables. Use this sauce to enhance your homemade pizzas and to create easy pasta dishes.

SALSA: Like marinara sauce, salsa comes in many intriguing varieties; why not choose something interesting, and not just medium or mild? Try smoky chipotle or cilantro-garlic. And for a real change of pace, try salsa verde, made of piquant tomatillos.

SOY SAUCE: Choose a good-quality, naturally brewed brand with reduced sodium content.

THAI PEANUT SATAY SAUCE: This sauce is not nearly as high in fat as it tastes, and it adds a blast of flavor to Thai-style dishes. I especially like to use it as a base for supereasy sauces and dressings, especially Coconut-Peanut Sauce or Salad Dressing (page 215).

PLUS A FEW ONCE-IN-A-WHILE ITEMS: In this category are a few items that you may enjoy using occasionally, but that don't necessarily need to be staples. These include Asian hoisin sauce, teriyaki sauce, Thai red or green curry paste, miso, and chutney.

Nuts, Nut Butters, and Seeds

Here's an underused food group. When vegans think of protein, our minds range over to soy products, and when we are really being sensible, to beans. But don't overlook nuts as a rich source of protein as well as valuable vitamins and minerals. A sprinkling of nuts goes a long way to boost the flavor and nutritional content of grain dishes, pastas, salads, stir-fries, and desserts.

    Nuts to keep on hand are cashews, almonds (whole nuts are

good for snacking; slivered or sliced work well in recipes), walnuts, pecans, and peanuts. Seeds you'll find useful are pumpkin, sunflower, and sesame. Pine nuts, used in several recipes in this book, are a rich treat on occasion. They're somewhat expensive and quite perishable, so buy small quantities, use soon after purchasing, and refrigerate whatever is not used at once. Note that pine nuts as well as other nuts and seeds freeze well.

Nut butters, too, deserve a prominent place in the pantry. Just be sure to use natural nut butters with no added fats, salt, sugar, or other questionable ingredients. Peanut butter and cashew butter are the ones used most often in these recipes.

Tofu, Tempeh, and Other Protein Products

TOFU: If you're a tofu fan, you'll want to keep a few varieties in your refrigerator. Those I can't live without are the standard 16-ounce tubs (both firm and extra-firm) and baked tofu (explore the Soy Boy and White Wave varieties—so many good ones to choose from). Keep a few 12.3-ounce aseptic packages of Mori-Nu firm and extra-firm silken tofu in your pantry as well.

TEMPEH: This fermented soy product comes in 8-ounce packages, in several varieties: plain soy, or soy plus grains, flax, veggies, and others. Truth be told, I don't find that the flavor differs much from one variety to another; I suppose the benefit is more from the nutrients that the additional ingredients lend to the mix. Fakin' Bacon smoky tempeh strips is another tempeh product I keep on hand most of the time. It's fantastic in wraps and sandwiches; I also use it in a couple of offbeat recipes in this book.

SEITAN: As mentioned in the introduction to Chapter Two, this product is pure wheat gluten, so it's not for those with any sort of wheat sensitivity. But for everyone else, seitan offers an appealing protein alternative to soy products. If you can make your own, so much the better. You'll find recipes in books and on the Web. It's not difficult, but rather time-consuming, even starting with the shortcut of using gluten flour. Second best is fresh seitan made by a local seitan-making outfit (now there's a growth industry!). Sometimes you'll find fresh seitan in food co-ops. Otherwise, the widely marketed White Wave seitan products found in natural foods stores (and increasingly, in supermarkets), including their stir-fry strips, are quite good.

TOFURKY SAUSAGE: Generally, I'm not that big on meat substitutes. Not that I'm against the concept; meat substitutes can help people transition to a less meat-centered diet and provide variety and convenience. However, I'm a little concerned about one of the primary ingredients in many of these products (which include deli slices, soy hot dogs, burger crumbles, and the like)—soy protein isolate. From what I know, this is a highly processed food, and not always listed in ingredients as organic. And while I found many, many more positive articles than negative while exploring information on soy protein, I would personally rather use soy products that are close to their actual food origin (such as tofu from soymilk, tempeh from whole soybeans, etc.) than more processed ones.

Tofurky brand sausages are especially appealing since they're made primarily of tofu and wheat gluten, and most of the ingredients listed are organic. They're delectably spicy, and can be used in a number of ways to make a quick, fun meal. Sliced and sautéed, they're great on pizza and in vegan jambalaya; or serve them simply sautéed on their own to add some bold-flavored protein to the plate. My family especially likes the Italian-flavored Tofurky sausage, though we've enjoyed the kielbasa style as well.

MY FAVORITE RECIPES This being my tenth cookbook and the culmination of a career of recipe testing and refining, I fully expected that an all-new book of uncomplicated, fresh dishes would be a challenge to produce. Still, I very much wanted to add a completely new, vegan book to my life's work. I did "veganize" an earlier book, *Vegetarian Soups for All Seasons,* for its third edition, though most of its recipes are not new. Indeed, I did have to stretch my culinary creativity, but fortunately, it was lots of fun, especially when I drew on inspiration gleaned from travels near (New York City, Boston, and Washington, D.C.) and far (Israel, Paris, and Amsterdam).

Considering how many recipes I've developed over the years, I was truly surprised at how many of these have become family favorites, ones that I make over and over again. They seem to please all the palates in our vegan family, and satisfy the considerable appetites of our two teenage sons. One more benefit to our vegan lifestyle is that all four members of my family are at an ideal weight, though we eat heartily. Actually, make that the five members of our family—our vegan cat, Jasmine, joins us at the table (or rather, under the table) almost every night for scraps. She especially likes peas, corn, and potatoes.

This was a roundabout way to bring you to the main point of this section. When I look at other authors' cookbooks, I often wonder which recipes they particularly like, but there's rarely a hint of what those may be. So, I thought it would be fun to share with you which recipes have become personal favorites from each chapter.

Chapter One: Speedy, Savory Soups
- Nearly Instant Thai Coconut Corn Soup (page 26)
- White Bean and Escarole Soup (page 33)

Chapter Two: The Protein Trio—Tofu, Tempeh, and Seitan
- Golden Tofu Triangles with Rich Peanut Sauce (page 46)
- Seitan and Polenta Skillet with Fresh Greens (page 64)

Now you know what my favorites are, and I hope that as you cook your way through this book, you'll let me know (nava@vegkitchen.com) what yours are, too.

Orzo Soup with Roasted Vegetables

Nearly Instant Thai Coconut Corn Soup

Curried Cashew and Green Pea Soup

Tofu Vegetable Soup with Bean Thread Noodles

Asian Noodle Soup with Bok Choy and Shiitake
    Mushrooms

Quick Green Veggie Soup with Couscous

Tomato Chickpea Soup with Tiny Pasta and Fresh
    Herbs

White Bean and Escarole Soup

Red Lentil Soup with Fresh Dill and Crisp Pita
    Croutons

Miso Soup with Sweet Potatoes and Watercress

Pink Bean, Quinoa, and Spinach Soup

Cool White Bean and Cucumber Soup

Fresh Tomato-Coconut Soup

CHAPTER ONE

Speedy, Savory Soups

I love few things better than preparing a long-simmering soup. As I write this, in fact, a snowstorm is falling, I'm stuck at home, and a pot of split pea soup has been on the stovetop for the better part of two hours.

Few days afford me the luxury of this kind of time, though I can usually find a one-hour window in which to make a good soup. Then again, there are those times when the craving for soup strikes, and dinnertime is looming. Rather than opening a can or doing without, I prefer making a nearly instant soup— one that requires little or no simmering to taste great, and whose prep and cooking can be completed within fifteen to thirty minutes. No need to sacrifice fresh vegetables in these kinds of soups, though I do often rely on prepared vegetable broth, a favorite shortcut in this category. Though many of the soups in this chapter can serve as the centerpiece of a meal, most pair well with other quick dishes like pizzas, wraps, or salads.

Orzo Soup with Roasted Vegetables

Orzo is a rice-shaped pasta. Look for the tricolor variety. While the orzo cooks, the vegetables for this soup roast in the oven, resulting in a sweet, smoky flavor when submerged in the broth.

6 SERVINGS

1 tablespoon olive oil, plus more for the pan

1 medium red bell pepper, diced

2 large celery stalks, sliced into 1$\frac{1}{2}$-inch-long pieces on the diagonal

8 baby carrots, quartered lengthwise

1 medium turnip, peeled and diced

1 cup sliced baby bella or cremini mushrooms

1 cup orzo

One 32-ounce carton low-sodium vegetable broth

2 to 3 tablespoons minced fresh dill

Salt and freshly ground pepper to taste

Calories: 158
Total fat: 3 g
Protein: 5 g
Carbohydrates: 28 g
Fiber: 2 g
Sodium: 285 mg

1   Preheat the oven to 425°F. Lightly oil a roasting pan.

2   Combine the bell pepper, celery, carrots, turnip, and mushrooms in a mixing bowl. Drizzle with the olive oil and stir together. Transfer the vegetables to the prepared pan. Roast for 20 minutes, or until the vegetables are touched with brown spots. Stir once or twice during this time.

3   Meanwhile, bring 3 cups water to a boil in a small pot. Add the orzo and simmer steadily until al dente, about 8 minutes (don't drain). Once the orzo is done, immediately pour in the vegetable broth and remove from the heat.

4   When the vegetables are done, stir them into the soup along with fresh dill to taste. Return to the heat until heated through. Season with salt and pepper and serve.

Menu suggestions

> A perfect partner for this soup is pizza, which can bake at the same time—and same temperature—as the veggies. Choose between White Pizza with Sweet Potato and Caramelized Onions (page 136) or Very Green Veggie Pesto Pizza (page 142).

> Wraps filled with a protein food and plenty of cool, raw vegetables provide a nice foil for the flavor and texture of this soup. Many of the ideas under Easy, Tasty Wraps (page 151) would work well—take your pick!

> For a soup-and-salad dinner, serve with Spinach, Artichoke, and Chickpea Salad (page 156) and fresh bread.

Nearly Instant Thai Coconut Corn Soup

When I first came up with this soup, I was looking to make something speedy to serve with a main dish salad. And speedy it is, taking only about fifteen minutes from start to finish, yet it tastes like a long-simmering soup. At first, I thought I was imagining things, but I've made it many times since, and that's just how long it takes. The tiny bit of red curry gives it ample heat; if you'd like a spicier soup, use more, and for a less spicy effect, omit the red curry altogether.

6 SERVINGS

1 tablespoon light olive oil

3 garlic cloves, minced

4 to 5 scallions, thinly sliced

1 medium red bell pepper, cut into short, narrow strips

Two 14- to 15-ounce cans light coconut milk

$1^{1}/_{2}$ cups rice milk

One 16-ounce bag frozen corn

2 teaspoons good-quality curry powder

$^{1}/_{4}$ teaspoon Thai red curry paste, or to taste

1 teaspoon salt, or to taste

$^{1}/_{2}$ cup minced fresh cilantro

Calories: 225
Total fat: 12 g
Protein: 3 g
Carbohydrates: 31 g
Fiber: 3 g
Sodium: 435 mg

1   Heat the oil in a small soup pot. Add the garlic, the white parts of the scallions, and the bell pepper. Sauté over medium-low heat until softened and golden, 2 to 3 minutes.

2   Add the coconut milk, rice milk, corn, curry powder, and the green parts of the scallions. If using the curry paste, dissolve it in a small amount of water before adding to the soup.

3   Bring to a rapid simmer, then lower the heat. Cover and simmer gently for 5 minutes. Season with salt and remove from the heat.

4   Serve, passing around the cilantro for topping.

Variation   If you have more time, this makes a wonderful cold summer soup. Do step 1, but don't heat after adding the coconut milk and rice milk in step 2. Use 4 to 5 ears lightly cooked fresh corn instead of frozen corn; rinse under cool water and scrape off the kernels. If you'd like, use minced fresh chiles instead of the curry paste. Refrigerate the soup until chilled.

Menu suggestions

> For a soup-and-salad meal, this pairs perfectly with Thai Tossed Salad (page 184).

> This soup is a good first course for Thai Steamed Green Garden with Coconut-Peanut Sauce (page 54). Serve with a platter of raw vegetables.

> I also recommend this soup to begin a meal of Gingery Rice with Sweet Potatoes and Peas (page 88). Start the rice dish first, as it takes longer to cook. Serve with a simple salad of mixed baby greens, tomatoes, and cucumbers.

Curried Cashew and Green Pea Soup

A delectable, high-protein puree made of cashew butter and silken tofu forms the base of this nearly instant soup. This soup is good warm, at room temperature, or even chilled, if you have the time to refrigerate it.

6 SERVINGS

2 cups rice milk

$1/2$ cup cashew butter

One 12.3-ounce package firm silken tofu

1 to 2 teaspoons good-quality curry powder

$1/2$ teaspoon minced fresh or jarred ginger

$1/2$ teaspoon dried dill

1 medium tomato, diced

3 cups frozen green peas, steamed

1 to 2 scallions, green parts only, minced

$1/4$ cup minced fresh cilantro

2 tablespoons lime juice

Salt and freshly ground pepper to taste

Calories: 260
Total fat: 13 g
Protein: 12 g
Carbohydrates: 27 g
Fiber: 5 g
Sodium: 135 g

1   Combine $1/2$ cup of the rice milk with the cashew butter and tofu in a food processor. Process until smoothly pureed.

2   To serve at room temperature, transfer the puree to a serving container, then stir in the rest of the rice milk and the remaining ingredients. Check the seasoning, then serve. To serve chilled, refrigerate the soup for an hour or so.

3   To serve warm, transfer the puree to a small soup pot. Add the rest of the rice milk and the remaining ingredients, stir together, and heat until just warmed through. Adjust the consistency with a little more rice milk if needed. Check the seasoning and serve.

Menu suggestions

> Served warm, there's something about this soup that calls for a hearty grain dish as a partner. I like it with Quinoa with Wild Mushrooms and Mixed Squashes (page 90). A simple green salad completes the meal.

> As a cool soup, it's delicious with Sweet and White Potato Salad with Mixed Greens (page 188). Add a simply prepared cauliflower dish like Sautéed Cauliflower with Sun-Dried Tomatoes and Basil (page 198) if you like.

> For a nice summer meal, serve with one or two lighter salads—many of those in Chapter Seven, Salads and Veggies on the Side, work well with this soup. Add some fresh bread or corn on the cob.

Tofu Vegetable Soup with Bean Thread Noodles

This Asian-style soup is ideal when you're in a hurry. It can be on the table in about twenty minutes.

1   In a heatproof container, combine the noodles with enough boiling water to cover. Let stand, covered, for 15 to 20 minutes, or until al dente. Drain well, then place on a cutting board and chop in several directions to shorten the noodles.

2   Meanwhile, combine the broth with 2 cups water in a soup pot. Bring to a simmer, then add the snow peas, bell pepper, spinach, tofu, ginger, and sesame oil. Cook briefly, just until the spinach is wilted and the soup is heated through.

3   Remove from the heat, stir in the noodles, and season with soy sauce and pepper to taste. Serve at once.

Menu suggestions

> This pairs nicely with Bok Choy, Edamame, Cashew, and Orange Rice (page 83). A platter of sliced bell peppers, daikon radish or turnip, and grape tomatoes or sliced tomatoes completes the meal.

> For a lighter meal, serve with store-bought vegan spring rolls and Bok Choy, Red Cabbage, and Carrot Salad (page 176).

4 TO 6 SERVINGS

One 3- to 4-ounce package bean thread (cellophane) noodles
One 32-ounce carton low-sodium vegetable broth
1 cup snow peas, cut in half
1/2 medium red or orange bell pepper, cut into thin strips
4 to 6 ounces baby spinach or arugula
One 16-ounce tub firm tofu, cut into 1/2-inch dice
2 teaspoons minced fresh or jarred ginger
1 teaspoon dark sesame oil
2 tablespoons reduced-sodium soy sauce, or to taste
Freshly ground pepper

Calories: 198
Total fat: 7.5 g
Protein: 14 g
Carbohydrates: 20 g
Fiber: 3 g
Sodium: 435 mg

Asian Noodle Soup with Bok Choy and Shiitake Mushrooms

Thick, hearty noodles make this fifteen-minute soup substantial, yet it's not too filling to serve as an introduction to another course.

6 SERVINGS

One 32-ounce carton low-sodium vegetable broth

One 9-ounce package fresh Asian noodles, or one 8-ounce package udon noodles

2 to 3 ounces fresh shiitake mushrooms, stemmed and sliced

1 to 2 teaspoons minced fresh or jarred ginger

4 large or 6 medium stalks bok choy, with leaves, sliced

3 to 4 scallions, sliced

2 to 3 tablespoons fresh cilantro leaves, optional

1 tablespoon reduced-sodium soy sauce, or to taste

Freshly ground pepper

Calories: 180
Total fat: 1.5 g
Protein: 7 g
Carbohydrates: 36 g
Fiber: 3.5 g
Sodium: 395 mg

1 Combine the broth with 2 cups water in a soup pot and bring to a rapid simmer.

2 Cut the fresh noodles into 2- to 3-inch lengths, or break the udon noodles into thirds. Add the noodles, mushrooms, and ginger to taste to the simmering broth. Cook until the noodles are al dente, 3 to 4 minutes.

3 Add the bok choy, scallions, and cilantro, and cook for just 2 to 3 minutes longer. Season with soy sauce and pepper to taste, then serve at once.

Menu suggestions

> This soup is a good first course to be followed by a tofu and tempeh dish. Try it with any of the following: Tofu and Seitan Mixed Grill (page 44), Tempeh Fries with Horseradish or Wasabi-Dill Mayonnaise (page 78), or Barbecue-Flavored Roasted Tempeh and Vegetables (page 79).

> As with the previous soup, store-bought spring rolls are a fun accompaniment. Continuing the meal with recipe-free accompaniments, follow with diced or sliced tofu or tempeh, sautéed in a little soy sauce and oil, steamed broccoli, and raw veggies or a simple salad of your choice.

Quick Green Veggie Soup with Couscous

For this bountiful vegetable soup, the less cooking time, the better. Everything should remain bright green and just tender-crisp.

1   In a small heatproof container, combine the couscous with 1 cup boiling water. Cover and set aside.

2   In a soup pot, combine the broth with 2 cups water and bring to a simmer. Add the zucchini, peas, broccoli, scallions, ginger to taste, and dill. Return to a rapid simmer, then cover and cook 3 to 4 minutes, until the vegetables are just done.

3   Stir in soy sauce to taste along with the oil, spinach, and parsley. Cook for another minute or two, just until the spinach has wilted.

4   Stir in the couscous. Season with pepper and, if desired, additional soy sauce. Serve at once.

Menu suggestions

This soup teams well with salad-filled wraps. I suggest making the wraps first, as the soup will need your full attention for the short time span it requires. Any of the following, from Easy, Tasty Wraps (page 151), will yield a delightful soup-and-wrap dinner: BBQ Seitan and Avocado Salad Wraps (page 152), Hummus and Avocado Wraps (page 152), or Baked Tofu and Raw Veggie Wraps (page 152).

6 SERVINGS

$1/2$ cup couscous, preferably whole wheat

One 32-ounce carton vegetable broth, preferably low-sodium

1 medium zucchini, quartered lengthwise and diced

$1/2$ cup frozen green peas or frozen edamame, completely thawed

$1^1/2$ cups finely chopped broccoli florets

3 scallions, sliced

1 to 2 teaspoons minced fresh or jarred ginger

2 tablespoons chopped fresh dill

2 to 3 tablespoons reduced-sodium soy sauce

1 tablespoon olive oil

2 to 3 ounces baby spinach or watercress

$1/4$ cup chopped fresh parsley or cilantro

Freshly ground pepper

Calories: 112
Total fat: 2.5 g
Protein: 4 g
Carbohydrates: 18 g
Fiber: 3 g
Sodium: 450 mg

Tomato Chickpea Soup with Tiny Pasta and Fresh Herbs

Here's a soup that comes together in no time, yet tastes as if it has been simmered for hours.

6 SERVINGS

2 tablespoons extra virgin olive oil

2 to 3 garlic cloves, minced

1 cup tiny pasta such as ditalini or bows

One 28-ounce can crushed tomatoes

One 15- to 16-ounce can chickpeas, drained and rinsed

2 teaspoons paprika

$1/4$ cup oil-packed sliced sun-dried tomatoes, optional

$1/4$ to $1/2$ cup sliced basil leaves, as desired

$1/4$ cup minced fresh parsley

2 tablespoons minced fresh dill, or more to taste

Salt and freshly ground pepper to taste

Calories: 180
Total fat: 8 g
Protein: 5 g
Carbohydrates: 24 g
Fiber: 7 g
Sodium: 210 mg

1   Heat the oil in a soup pot. Add the garlic and sauté over low heat until golden.

2   Add 4 cups water. Bring to a rapid simmer, then stir in the pasta. Cook according to package directions until just al dente.

3   Add the remaining ingredients, except the salt and pepper. Return to a simmer, then cover and simmer gently for 8 minutes. Season with salt and pepper, then serve.

Menu suggestions

> This soup pairs wonderfully with white pizza. Depending on the season, serve it with White Pizza with Sweet Potato and Caramelized Onions (page 136) or White Pizza with Asparagus and Spinach (page 138).

> This also goes nicely with Red and Green Cashew Butter Wraps (page 153) or Tempeh Bacon, Portobello Mushroom, and Coleslaw Wraps (page 153).

> A light and colorful companion salad is Broccoli Salad with Yellow Peppers, Pine Nuts, and Cranberries (page 182). Serve the soup and salad with fresh bread or corn on the cob.

White Bean and Escarole Soup

Oh, how I adore this soup, which I discovered at The Bakery in New Paltz, New York. A simple Italian classic, this soup has a number of variations, but I find there's no need to dress up the basic formula. Escarole is a sturdy green that's too tough for many salads, but it cooks quickly and, combined with cannellini beans, gives an almost buttery scent and flavor to the soup.

1   Heat the oil in a soup pot. Add the onion and sauté over medium heat until translucent. Add the garlic and continue to sauté, stirring frequently, until both are golden.

2   Add the broth and beans, turn up the heat, and bring to a rapid simmer. Stir in the escarole and half of the parsley, lower the heat, cover, and simmer gently for 8 to 10 minutes, until the escarole is tender.

3   Stir in additional water as needed. The soup should be dense, but not overly so. Return to a simmer. Stir in the remaining parsley, season with salt and pepper, and serve.

Menu suggestions

> For a simple, light meal, serve with fresh bread and one of the Recipe Not Required mixed greens salads (page 192).

> For a heartier meal, serve with Zucchini and Polenta Marinara (page 200) and a platter of raw vegetables and olives.

> See the menu with Pasta Puttanesca (page 133).

6 SERVINGS

2 tablespoons extra virgin olive oil

1 medium onion, quartered and thinly sliced

2 to 3 garlic cloves, minced

One 32-ounce carton low-sodium vegetable broth

Two 16-ounce cans cannellini beans, drained and rinsed

1 medium head (6 to 8 ounces) escarole, coarsely chopped and rinsed

1/2 cup chopped fresh parsley

Salt and freshly ground pepper to taste

Calories: 183
Total fat: 5 g
Protein: 6.5 g
Carbohydrates: 26 g
Fiber: 7 g
Sodium: 460 mg

Red Lentil Soup with Fresh Dill and Crisp Pita Croutons

My older son loves a very simple red lentil soup served at a local Middle Eastern café. It's good, but to my mind, not very interesting, so I created my own version, with a little more style and substance. I make this regularly and he rarely clamors for the café version.

6 SERVINGS

3 fresh pita breads, preferably whole grain, cut into small squares

1 1/2 tablespoons olive oil

2 medium onions, chopped

4 garlic cloves, minced

2 cups red lentils, rinsed

2 natural, salt-free vegetable bouillon cubes

2 teaspoons salt-free seasoning mix (such as Spike or Mrs. Dash)

4 to 6 ounces baby spinach or arugula

1/4 cup minced fresh dill

Salt and freshly ground pepper to taste

Calories: 345
Total fat: 5 g
Protein: 20 g
Carbohydrates: 58 g
Fiber: 13 g
Sodium: 255 mg

1   Preheat the oven or a toaster oven to 300°F.

2   Arrange the pita squares on a small baking sheet and bake until crisp, 10 to 15 minutes.

3   Heat the oil in a soup pot. Add the onions and sauté over medium heat until translucent. Add the garlic and continue to sauté until both are golden.

4   Add 6 cups water, followed by the lentils, bouillon cubes, and seasoning mix. Bring to a rapid simmer, then lower the heat, cover, and simmer gently until the lentils are mushy, about 25 minutes.

5   Remove from the heat and insert an immersion blender. Process until the soup is smoothly pureed. Or, let cool slightly, then puree the soup in batches in a food processor.

6   If the soup is too thick, adjust the consistency with a bit more water. Return to low heat and stir in the spinach and dill. Cook just until piping hot. Season with salt and pepper, garnish with the pita squares, and serve.

Menu suggestions

> With this soup, I often continue the Middle Eastern theme and serve it with Middle Eastern Chopped Salad (page 191), more fresh pita bread, and hummus or baba ghanouj (store-bought or homemade).

> This also goes well with cauliflower dishes, hot or cold—Quinoa with Cauliflower, Cranberries, and Pine Nuts (page 92), Sautéed Cauliflower with Sun-Dried Tomatoes and Basil (page 198), or Cauliflower and Carrot Salad (page 188). With any of these choices, a platter of diced tomatoes and cucumbers drizzled with olive oil and lemon juice completes the meal.

Miso Soup with Sweet Potatoes and Watercress

Miso and watercress are both splendid sources of vitamin C; they team up in this quick soup to great effect. As I mention in the ingredient list, I like this with a dark, robust variety of miso such as barley or hatcho.

6 SERVINGS

2 medium sweet potatoes

2 natural, salt-free vegetable bouillon cubes

One 12.3-ounce package firm or extra-firm silken tofu, finely diced

1 bunch watercress, thinly sliced

3 to 4 scallions, thinly sliced

2 teaspoons minced fresh or jarred ginger

2 to 4 tablespoons dark miso, such as barley or hatcho

Freshly ground pepper

Calories: 95
Total fat: 2.5 g
Protein: 6 g
Carbohydrates: 12 g
Fiber: 1 g
Sodium: 280 mg

1   Microwave the sweet potatoes until done but still firm, starting with 2 minutes per potato. Plunge into a bowl of ice water.

2   Pour 5 cups water into a soup pot; add the bouillon cubes and bring to a rapid simmer. Add the tofu, watercress, scallions, and ginger. Stir gently, return to a rapid simmer, then remove from heat.

3   Peel the sweet potatoes and cut into small dice. Stir into the soup.

4   Dissolve 2 tablespoons of miso in a small amount of warm water. Add to the soup and taste. If you'd like a saltier, more pungent taste, add another tablespoon or two of miso dissolved in a little warm water. Season with pepper to taste and serve at once.

Menu suggestions

> For a light soup-and-wrap meal, serve this with Baked Tofu and Raw Veggie Wraps (page 152).

> Suitable soup-and-salad pairings include Tropical Tofu Salad with Chutney Mayonnaise (page 157) and Asian Edamame and Tofu Chopped Salad (page 158).

> Serve this soup as a first course for a noodle dish. Try Seitan Chow Fun (page 120) or Soba Noodles with Green Beans and Almonds (page 127). Add Bok Choy, Red Cabbage, and Carrot Salad (176) or any simple salad of your choice.

Pink Bean, Quinoa, and Spinach Soup

An appetizing, mildly spiced mélange of nourishing beans, grains, and greens, this makes a stellar centerpiece for a soup-based meal. Quinoa is an excellent source of protein, making this practically a meal in a bowl.

1 Heat the oil in a large soup pot. Add the onion and sauté over medium-low heat until translucent. Add the carrots and garlic and continue to sauté until all are golden, about 5 minutes.

2 Add 6 cups water, followed by the bouillon cubes, tomatoes, quinoa, beans, curry powder, cinnamon, and nutmeg. Bring to a rapid simmer, then cover and simmer gently for 15 to 20 minutes, until the quinoa is tender.

3 Add the spinach and cover. Cook for just a minute or two, until it is wilted, then stir it into the soup. Adjust the consistency with a little more water if the soup is too dense; season with salt and pepper and serve.

Menu suggestions

> For a delicious soup-and-salad meal, pair this with Mixed Greens with Sprouts, Apple, and Daikon (page 179) and serve with fresh whole-grain olive bread or a fresh flatbread such as pita or lavash.

> To complete the meal without using further recipes, serve with vegan cheese quesadillas (use a griddle on the stovetop or bake in a 400°F oven) or simple nachos (tortilla chips topped with melted vegan cheese and, if you'd like, some green chiles), and a salad of mixed greens, tomatoes, peppers, and olives.

6 OR MORE SERVINGS

1½ tablespoons extra virgin olive oil
1 medium onion, finely chopped
8 baby carrots, quartered lengthwise
2 garlic cloves, minced
2 natural, salt-free vegetable bouillon cubes
One 14- to 16-ounce can diced tomatoes
½ cup quinoa, rinsed in a fine sieve
One 15- to 16-ounce can pink beans, drained and rinsed
2 teaspoons good-quality curry powder
Pinch of ground cinnamon
Pinch of ground nutmeg
5 to 6 ounces baby spinach rinsed
Salt and freshly ground pepper to taste

Calories: 181
Total fat: 5 g
Protein: 7.5 g
Carbohydrates: 26 g
Fiber: 6 g
Sodium: 280 mg

Cool White Bean and Cucumber Soup

With a few choice ingredients and just minutes, you've got a substantial soup for a summer day. Choose a crisp, flavorful cucumber with pale green (rather than watery white) flesh for optimal flavor. If the cucumber is organic and unwaxed, leave the peel on for extra fiber and flavor. If you have more time, cover and refrigerate the soup for an hour or more before serving.

6 SERVINGS

Two 15- to 16-ounce cans cannellini or Great Northern beans, drained and rinsed

3 cups rice milk, plus more if needed

1 large cucumber, peeled or not, as desired

4 to 6 radishes, halved and sliced

1/4 cup minced fresh dill

2 scallions, green parts only, thinly sliced

Juice of 1 lemon

Salt and freshly ground pepper to taste

Vegan Sour Cream (page 213), optional

Calories: 230
Total fat: 2 g
Protein: 11 g
Carbohydrates: 44 g
Fiber: 7 g
Sodium: 50 mg

1   Combine half of the beans with 1 cup of the rice milk in a food processor. Process until smoothly pureed, then transfer to a serving container. Stir in the remaining rice milk and beans.

2   Quarter the cucumber lengthwise. Cut away and discard the seeds, then slice thinly and add to the serving container.

3   Stir in the radishes, dill, scallions, and lemon juice. If the soup is too thick, adjust the consistency with a little more rice milk. Season with salt and pepper. If you'd like, top each serving with a dollop of Vegan Sour Cream.

Menu suggestions

> See the menu with Roasted Summer Vegetable Platter (page 162).

> For a cool, stove-free summer meal, serve with Baked Tofu and Raw Veggie Wraps (page 152) or Red and Green Cashew Butter Wraps (page 153).

Fresh Tomato-Coconut Soup

I love making cool, refreshing soups that need no cooking at all on hot summer days. This one is nothing like the classic Indian soup of the same name, but it has a personality all its own. For best results, use the most flavorful, lush summer tomatoes available.

1 Combine the tomatoes, scallions, and dill in a food processor. Process until coarsely pureed, then transfer to a serving container.

2 Whisk in the coconut milk, lime juice, paprika, salt, and pepper. Cover and let the soup stand, either at room temperature or refrigerated, for 15 minutes or so to allow the flavors to blend.

3 To serve, ladle the soup into bowls, then place a little of each topping ingredient in the center of each bowl. Serve at once.

Menu suggestions

This soup is nice served side by side with a cool noodle dish or a main dish salad. It pairs well with any of the following: fresh corn on the cob, steamed broccoli, or green beans. Complete a meal with any of the following choices: Southeast Asian Cold Noodles with Tempeh (page 166), Tropical Tofu Salad with Chutney Mayonnaise (page 157), Gado Gado (page 160), or Asian Edamame and Tofu Chopped Salad (page 158).

6 SERVINGS

2 pounds tomatoes, coarsely chopped
2 scallions, green parts only, coarsely chopped
2 to 3 tablespoons fresh dill or cilantro leaves
One 14- to 15-ounce can light coconut milk
Juice of 1 lime, or more to taste
1 teaspoon sweet paprika
Salt and freshly ground pepper to taste

For topping
1 large yellow tomato, finely diced
¹/₂ cup cooked chickpeas
¹/₄ cup finely diced orange or green bell pepper
6 to 8 fresh basil leaves, cut into strips

Calories: 113
Total fat: 5 g
Protein: 3 g
Carbohydrates: 17 g
Fiber: 3 g
Sodium: 25 g

CHAPTER TWO

The Protein Trio—Tofu, Tempeh, and Seitan

In the veg world, tofu, tempeh, and seitan are regarded as the protein powerhouses (though in all fairness, beans and whole grains perform a similar function). All are such staples in our home that if any are missing from the refrigerator, I know it's time to go shopping. On my must-have list are always the quivering white blocks of tofu (both firm and extra-firm) that strike fear into the hearts of non–tofu eaters and aseptic packages of firm silken tofu, as well as flavorful baked tofu.

Tempeh is an acquired taste, and I have to admit that in my family, only my older son and I are big fans; my younger son tolerates it, and my husband doesn't care for it at all. You'll see that this chapter is more weighted toward tofu for this very reason, and also because, of these two soy products, tofu is the more versatile. Still, tempeh is a bold and fascinating food, and for those who do have a taste for it, it's worth using regularly.

As far as seitan goes, I can only speak from my own experience, but everyone I've introduced it to has been delighted and amazed. Former meat eaters swear by its meatiness, and current meat eaters promise that if I come over and cook seitan for them every day, they will give up meat. I'm still trying to convince them that they, too, can make seitan dishes, all by themselves. The only caveat for seitan is that it is not for those with gluten sensitivity, as that is what seitan is— pure wheat gluten.

Because the protein foods in this trio come practically ready to eat, they're a boon for making express meals. Many of this book's readers will already know plenty about what to do with tofu, tempeh, and seitan. So, what I've aimed for here is to present recipes that you don't see all over the place. I hope you will find them to be deliciously different from what you're already familiar with.

Mediterranean Tofu

A hot day, a big bunch of basil, and some great local tomatoes—all these came together a few summers ago to inspire a Mediterranean-flavored twist for tofu. This is a splendid main dish for warm summer evenings.

4 SERVINGS

Two 16-ounce tubs firm tofu
2 tablespoons extra virgin olive oil
4 garlic cloves, minced
2 cups finely diced tomatoes
1/4 cup oil-packed sun-dried tomatoes, cut into strips, with a little of their oil
2 tablespoons lemon juice, or to taste
Salt and freshly ground pepper to taste
Fresh basil leaves, cut into strips

Calories: 415
Total fat: 25 g
Protein: 38 g
Carbohydrates: 19 g
Fiber: 7 g
Sodium: 80 mg

1   Cut each block of tofu into 6 equal slabs. Blot well between layers of clean tea towels or paper towels.

2   Heat 1 tablespoon of the oil in a griddle or extra-wide skillet. Arrange the slabs of tofu in a single layer and cook over medium-high heat until golden on both sides, 5 to 7 minutes per side.

3   Meanwhile, heat the remaining tablespoon of oil in a smaller skillet. Add the garlic and sauté over low heat until golden. Add the fresh and dried tomatoes and lemon juice. Cook over medium heat until the fresh tomato has just softened and is heated through, about 2 minutes. Season with salt and pepper.

4   To serve, fan out 3 slices of tofu on each plate and spoon some of the tomato-garlic sauce over them. Top each serving with a few strips of basil, then serve at once.

Menu suggestions

> For a light summer meal, this dish goes nicely with a substantial salad. Try it with either Herb Garden Couscous and Black Bean Salad (page 164) or Spinach, Artichoke, and Chickpea Salad (page 156).

> Good pastas to pair this with include Pasta Twists with Cauliflower and Spinach (page 126) and Creamy Pasta with Asparagus and Peas (page 128).

> To complete the meal with few or no further recipes, serve with a bountiful green salad of your choice or one of the Recipe Not Required suggestions for mixed greens salads on page 192; add fresh bread and corn on the cob to complete the meal.

Tofu and Seitan Mixed Grill

On a visit to Israel, I came across a convenient vegan product called "mixed grill"—thin strips of tofu and seitan packaged together. Once home, I took this inspiration to create a simple, high-protein skillet dish.

4 SERVINGS

2 tablespoons olive oil

1 large onion, quartered and thinly sliced

One 16-ounce tub firm or extra-firm tofu

One 8-ounce package seitan, cut into bite-size strips

2 scallions, minced

Easy Gravy (page 218)

Calories: 348
Total fat: 18 g
Protein: 35 g
Carbohydrates: 16 g
Fiber: 5 g
Sodium: 655 mg

1   Heat 1 tablespoon of the oil in a wide skillet. Add the onion and sauté over medium-low heat until just beginning to brown, stirring frequently.

2   Meanwhile, cut the tofu into 6 slabs crosswise. Blot well between layers of paper towels or clean tea towels, then cut each slab into strips.

3   Transfer the onion to a plate and set aside. Heat the remaining tablespoon of oil in the same skillet and add the tofu and seitan. Sauté over medium-high heat until much of it is golden.

4   Return the onion to the skillet and add the scallions. Sauté for another minute or two, stirring frequently. Remove from the heat and cover to keep warm.

5   Prepare the gravy according to directions. Pour over the tofu-seitan mixture in the skillet, stir to combine, then return to the heat. Cook for a minute or so, stirring constantly, then serve at once.

Menu suggestions

Serve with hot cooked grains (brown rice, couscous, or bulgur). Broccoli Salad with Yellow Peppers, Pine Nuts, and Cranberries (page 182) or one of the mixed greens salads suggested in Recipe Not Required (page 192) completes the meal.

Tofu Shakshouka

Common to many regional Middle Eastern cuisines, this is one of those supersimple dishes that, with the right ingredients, is amazingly tasty. Especially welcome as a fast summer dish, this is a good showcase for the abundance of delicious tomatoes in season. Shakshouka, in its original version, is made with eggs; in this vegan rendition, only one change needs to be made—silken tofu replaces the eggs.

1   Heat the oil in a large skillet. Add the onion and sauté over medium-low heat until translucent. Add the bell pepper and continue to sauté until both are lightly browned.

2   Add the tofu, tomatoes, paprika, and turmeric. Stir together, then cook over medium heat for 10 to 15 minutes, until the tomatoes are soft. Season with salt and pepper, stir in the parsley, if using, and serve.

Variation   Some traditional recipes include garlic; add a few cloves of minced garlic with the bell pepper if you'd like a garlicky version.

Menu suggestions

> Make this the start of a delicious Middle Eastern–themed meal. Serve with hummus (store-bought or homemade), fresh pita bread, and Middle Eastern Chopped Salad (page 191).

> You can create a brunchlike meal (for any time of day) with Sautéed Paprika Potatoes (page 207) or Fingerling Fries (page 194), whole-grain toast, and sliced oranges.

4 TO 6 SERVINGS

2 tablespoons olive oil
1 large onion, finely chopped
1 medium green bell pepper, diced
Two 12.3-ounce packages firm silken tofu, finely crumbled
4 large or 6 medium tomatoes, diced
1 teaspoon sweet paprika
Pinch of turmeric, for color
Salt and freshly ground pepper to taste
2 tablespoons minced fresh parsley, optional

Calories: 230
Total fat: 12 g
Protein: 14 g
Carbohydrates: 19 g
Fiber: 3 g
Sodium: 75 mg

Golden Tofu Triangles with Rich Peanut Sauce

Amsterdam is host to a number of Indonesian restaurants (Indonesia was once a Dutch colony), and on a visit to this charming city with my sons, we were informed that a *rijkstaffel* ("rice table") meal would be a memorable experience. A big bowl of rice is served with several tasty little dishes. My sons were especially keen on the golden sautéed tofu on skewers that was accompanied by a rich peanut sauce.

Once home, I tried to reproduce the flavors of the luscious sauce to serve with triangles of sautéed tofu. Though my version is likely not truly authentic, what counts is that it tastes good, it's easy, and my sons are still crazy about it. Each time I make it, we're transported back to Amsterdam, if only briefly.

6 SERVINGS

Two 16-ounce tubs extra-firm tofu
1 tablespoon olive oil
Salt
Rich Peanut Sauce (page 214)

Calories: 262
Total fat: 19 g
Protein: 19 g
Carbohydrates: 9 g
Fiber: 1 g
Sodium: 250 mg

1   Cut each block of tofu into 6 slabs crosswise. Blot well with tea towels or paper towels, then cut each slab in half to make 2 squares. Finally, cut each square on the diagonal to make triangles.

2   Spread the oil evenly over the surface of a wide skillet and heat. Add the tofu and sauté over medium-high heat until golden on both sides, 10 to 15 minutes. Sprinkle with a little salt.

3   Meanwhile, prepare the sauce according to the recipe.

4   To serve, arrange some of the tofu triangles on each plate and drizzle with the sauce. Or, for a fun effect, thread the triangles onto skewers, then spoon the sauce over them.

Menu suggestions

> The traditional accompaniment to this is, of course, lots of cooked rice, but I also like it with bean thread (cellophane) noodles, rice vermicelli, or soba. If I'm not feeling too rushed, I like to thread a few tofu triangles on each of several skewers, then nestle the skewers on a bed of noodles. A steamed green vegetable (broccoli, asparagus, or Brussels sprouts, depending on the season) adds color to the plate.

> A good salad to accompany this is Mixed Greens with Sprouts, Apple, and Daikon (page 179) or Bok Choy, Red Cabbage, and Carrot Salad (page 176). Or, a platter of raw vegetables will do nicely in place of a salad.

Spicy Tofu Triangles on a Cool Bed of Lettuce

The contrast of warm, spicy tofu with cool, crisp lettuce is enticing. I use Nasoya Creamy Dill dressing, but any vegan ranch-style dressing, homemade or store-bought, will work. I use two pounds of tofu because of my ravenous teens, but if you're serving three or four "normal" eaters, one pound may suffice. Cut the rest of the ingredients in half as well.

4 TO 6 SERVINGS

Two 16-ounce tubs firm or extra-firm tofu

$1/4$ cup hoisin sauce

$1/4$ cup good-quality ketchup (see Note)

1 tablespoon reduced-sodium soy sauce

1 tablespoon agave nectar or maple syrup

2 tablespoons light olive oil

$1/4$ to $1/2$ teaspoon Thai red curry paste, to taste, dissolved in a small amount of warm water

2 to 3 cups thinly shredded crisp lettuce (such as romaine)

2 to 3 tablespoons vegan creamy dill or ranch dressing, as needed

Thinly sliced scallions or basil leaves, optional

Calories: 454
Total fat: 24 g
Protein: 37 g
Carbohydrates: 48 g
Fiber: 6 g
Sodium: 655 mg

1   Cut each block of tofu into 6 slabs crosswise. Blot well between tea towels or paper towels, then cut each slab in half to make 2 squares. Finally, cut each square on the diagonal to make triangles.

2   Combine the hoisin sauce, ketchup, soy sauce, agave nectar, oil, and dissolved curry paste in a small mixing bowl and whisk together.

3   Pour half of the sauce into an extra-wide skillet and heat gently. Add the tofu and pour the rest of the sauce over the top. Turn the heat to medium high. Cook, stirring frequently, for 15 to 20 minutes, until the sauce is completely reduced and the tofu begins to brown.

4   Toss the lettuce with the dressing. Allowing about $1/2$ cup of lettuce per serving, place a bed of lettuce on each plate and top with several tofu triangles. Garnish with some thinly sliced scallions or basil if desired.

Note Choose an all-natural brand of ketchup—not one loaded with sugar or high-fructose corn syrup.

Menu suggestions

> I like this with a light grain dish like Lemony Couscous with Broccoli (page 94) or Quinoa with Corn and Scallions (page 91). In either case, a simple green salad completes the meal.

> This is also nice with potato-based salads such as Sweet and White Potato Salad with Mixed Greens (page 188) or Warm Mediterranean Potato Salad (page 193).

> To complete the meal with no further formal recipes, choose one of the ideas for Easy Ways to Dress Up Pasta and Noodle Side Dishes (page 121) and one of the Recipe Not Required suggestions for mixed greens salads (192) or any simple green salad of your choice.

Stovetop Tofu Skewers

Serving tofu and veggies kebab-style is festive, but firing up the grill, marinating the ingredients, and soaking the bamboo skewers (so they don't ignite) can be time-consuming. And most people don't own a stovetop grill. Here's a shortcut method that circumvents all those steps, made right on an ordinary griddle.

4 SERVINGS

One 16-ounce tub extra-firm tofu

1 small green bell pepper, cut into 1-inch pieces

1 small red, orange, or yellow bell pepper, cut into 1-inch pieces

1 cup cherry or grape tomatoes

1 cup small baby bella or crimini mushrooms

1 1/2 tablespoons olive oil

2 1/2 tablespoons reduced-sodium soy sauce

2 tablespoons dry red or white wine

1/2 teaspoon dried basil

Calories: 185
Total fat: 12 g
Protein: 13 g
Carbohydrates: 8 g
Fiber: 2 g
Sodium: 355 mg

1   Cut the tofu into 4 thick slabs crosswise. Blot well between paper towels.

2   Alternate the chunks of tofu, bell peppers, tomatoes, and mushrooms on each of 8 bamboo skewers, leaving about 1 1/2 inches of skewer at the bottom, and filling the entire skewer as close as possible to the top. Wrap the open ends of the skewers with aluminum foil.

3   Combine the oil, soy sauce, wine, and basil in a small bowl and stir together. Heat half of the mixture on a griddle (either round or square) on the stovetop.

4   Arrange 4 of the skewers on the griddle, with the longer wrapped ends hanging off the edge. Cook over medium-high heat, turning frequently, for 8 to 10 minutes total, or until the tofu and vegetables are touched with golden brown spots here and there. Remove the skewers to a plate and cover with foil to keep warm while repeating with the remaining skewers.

Menu suggestions

> Arrange the skewers over a hot cooked grain (brown rice, couscous, quinoa, or a combination of quinoa and bulgur, which can cook together). Serve with steamed broccoli or cauliflower and a colorful salad.

> Serve with Sautéed Paprika Potatoes (page 207) and any of the Recipe Not Required ideas for mixed greens (page 192).

> This is also lovely with Sweet and White Potato Salad with Mixed Greens (page 188) and steamed green beans or asparagus.

Thai Tofu with Pineapple and Veggies

This is a nice change of pace from more common soy sauce–flavored stir-fries, but it's just as quick and every bit as delectable. Don't be alarmed by the ingredient list, which is relatively long compared with those in most recipes in this book. It really is a quick dish, and with such an array of healthy components, you'll need little else to make a satisfying meal.

4 TO 6 SERVINGS

One 16-ounce tub extra-firm tofu

2 tablespoons olive oil

1 tablespoon reduced-sodium soy sauce

1 medium onion, quartered and thinly sliced

8 baby carrots, halved lengthwise

1 cup frozen green peas

One 15- to 16-ounce can pineapple chunks or slices, drained (reserve juice for a different use)

One 15-ounce can baby corn, undrained

1 cup diced tomatoes

1 cup light coconut milk

2 stalks lemongrass, cut into thirds and bruised, optional

2 teaspoons good-quality curry powder, or to taste

2 tablespoons cornstarch

1/4 to 1 teaspoon red or green curry paste, optional

1/4 cup minced fresh cilantro

Salt to taste

Hot cooked grain (rice, quinoa, or couscous)

Calories: 322
Total fat: 14 g
Protein: 15 g
Carbohydrates: 40 g
Fiber: 14 g
Sodium: 500 mg

1 Cut the tofu into 6 slabs crosswise. Blot well on paper towels, then cut into dice.

2 Heat 1 tablespoon of the oil with the soy sauce in a stir-fry pan. Add the tofu and stir-fry over medium-high heat until golden on most sides, about 10 minutes. Transfer to a plate and set aside.

3 Heat the remaining tablespoon of oil in the same pan. Add the onion and carrots and sauté over medium heat for 5 minutes.

4 Add the peas, pineapple, baby corn, tomatoes, coconut milk, optional lemongrass, and curry powder. Gently stir in the tofu. Bring to a simmer, then cook for 5 minutes.

5 Combine the cornstarch and optional curry paste in a cup or small bowl. Add enough water to dissolve, then pour the mixture into the pan. Simmer gently until the liquid has thickened.

6 Stir in the cilantro and season with salt. Serve at once in shallow bowls over plenty of hot cooked grain.

Variation Try substituting a leek for the onion in this dish. Use the white portion of a medium or large leek; cut in half lengthwise, then slice into $^{1}/_{4}$-inch half-circles. Rinse well in a colander before using.

Menu suggestions

As mentioned in the headnote, this is a plentiful dish, so an interesting salad is enough to complete the meal. Two good choices are Bok Choy, Red Cabbage, and Carrot Salad (page 176) or Spinach and Red Cabbage Salad with Oranges and Almonds (page 180). Try the latter with the Sesame-Ginger Salad Dressing (page 222) option. If you'd like a little something extra with the meal, add prepared vegan dumplings or spring rolls (from your grocer's frozen foods section).

Thai Steamed Green Garden with Coconut-Peanut Sauce

Offering an attractive presentation of steamed fresh veggies, this is a nice change of pace from stir-fries. It's a fresh-tasting meal that gets its personality from a luscious sauce.

4 TO 6 SERVINGS

1 recipe Coconut-Peanut Sauce or Salad Dressing (page 215)

2 large broccoli crowns, cut into bite-size florets

8 ounces slender green beans (see Note), cut in half

2 stalks lemongrass, cut in half, optional

1 medium zucchini, halved lengthwise and sliced

1 red or orange bell pepper, cut into narrow strips

2 scallions, cut into 1-inch lengths

Two 8-ounce packages White Wave Thai-flavored baked tofu, cut into narrow strips

Salt to taste

Hot cooked rice

Calories: 440
Total fat: 23 g
Protein: 25 g
Carbohydrates: 35 g
Fiber: 23 g
Sodium: 880 mg

1 Prepare the sauce according to the recipe. Leave it at room temperature or heat until just warm if desired; set aside until needed.

2 In a wide skillet or stir-fry pan, combine the broccoli florets and green beans with just enough water to keep the bottom of the pan moist.

3 If using the lemongrass, bruise each section by creating long slits with a sharp knife. Lay them over the vegetables in the pan. Cover and steam until the broccoli and beans are just beginning to turn bright green, 5 to 7 minutes.

4 Add the zucchini, bell pepper, scallions, and tofu. Give the mixture a good stir, cover, and continue to steam until the vegetables are all tender-crisp, another 2 to 3 minutes. Season lightly with salt.

5 Serve at once with or over hot cooked rice. Pass the sauce in a spouted cup so everyone can use as much as they like.

Note When good fresh green beans are not in season, use frozen organic whole baby green beans.

Menu suggestions

This one-dish meal can be finished without much further ado. When I'm in a rush, I like this with rice-stick noodles; with a little more time to spare, it's delicious with brown basmati or forbidden black rice (a medium-size, nutty variety that's actually more purple than black). Either way, complete the meal with a platter of yellow cherry or grape tomatoes, chunks of mango and/or canned or fresh pineapple, and baby corn.

Szechuan-Style Tofu with Eggplant

This recipe is based on one of my favorite Chinese take-out dishes. The problem with the restaurant version is that it is often rather oily. I've devised this low-fat version as a way to satisfy my craving for it.

6 SERVINGS

1 tablespoon olive or peanut oil
1 teaspoon dark sesame oil
1 small onion, minced
4 to 5 garlic cloves, minced
2 long Japanese eggplants or 1 medium eggplant, about 1 pound total
One 16-ounce tub extra-firm tofu
$1/4$ cup dry white or red wine
$1/4$ cup hoisin sauce
2 teaspoons grated fresh or jarred ginger, or more to taste
4 large stalks bok choy or celery, thinly sliced on the diagonal
1 tablespoon soy sauce, or more to taste
Hot chile oil or Thai red curry paste

Calories: 155
Total fat: 8 g
Protein: 9 g
Carbohydrates: 13 g
Fiber: 2 g
Sodium: 270 mg

1   Heat the olive and sesame oils in a stir-fry pan. Add the onion and garlic and sauté over medium-low heat until golden.

2   Meanwhile, cut the Japanese eggplants into $1/4$-inch-thick slices. If using regular eggplant, quarter it lengthwise, then cut into $1/4$-inch-thick slices.

3   Cut the tofu into 6 slabs crosswise. Blot well with paper towels, then cut into narrow strips.

4   Add the eggplant and tofu to the pan, followed by the wine, hoisin sauce, ginger, and $1/4$ cup water. Cook, covered, over medium heat for 5 minutes, or until the eggplant is nearly tender. Lift the lid once or twice during that time to stir. Cook, uncovered, for 5 minutes longer, or until the liquid has been completely reduced.

5   Add the bok choy and stir-fry, uncovered, for just a minute or two, until warmed. Season to taste with soy sauce and chile oil. Serve at once.

Menu suggestions

> It's nice to serve this hearty dish over cooked quick grains (like whole-wheat couscous or quinoa) or Asian noodles. Or, if you have the time, cook some brown rice—that's how I like it best. Since this isn't a colorful dish, you'll need something to liven up the plate. Broccoli with Pine Nuts or Almonds (page 204) or Stir-Fried Baby Carrots (page 206) would be a good choice. A few cherry or grape tomatoes or pickled beets add interest to the plate as well.

> If you'd prefer something raw and crunchy to go with this, choose Bok Choy, Red Cabbage, and Carrot Salad (page 176), Fruitful Red Slaw (page 177), or Mixed Greens with Sprouts, Apple, and Daikon (page 179). A bed of noodles or grain would be welcome with this menu, too.

Tofu Rancheros

Years ago, on a trip to the Southwest, my husband and I (then vegetarians, not yet vegans) discovered the famous breakfast dish of the region and were quickly hooked. Huevos rancheros are scrambled eggs perched atop corn tortillas and topped with an incendiary sauce. It's easy to veganize this classic, as I've done here. Like the next recipe, this can be served for breakfast, brunch, lunch, or dinner.

4 SERVINGS

One 16-ounce tub firm tofu

3 tablespoons cornmeal

$2^1/_2$ tablespoons olive oil

Salt

1 medium onion, quartered and thinly sliced

1 medium green bell pepper, cut into short, narrow strips

1 small fresh chile pepper, seeds removed, minced, optional

One 16-ounce jar prepared salsa, any favorite variety

1 cup salt-free canned crushed tomatoes

8 corn tortillas

$1^1/_2$ cups grated vegan Cheddar or nacho cheese, optional

Calories: 569
Total fat: 33 g
Protein: 26 g
Carbohydrates: 50 g
Fiber: 13 g
Sodium: 1260 mg

1 Cut the tofu into 6 slabs crosswise. Blot well between paper towels or clean tea towels, then cut into small dice.

2 Combine the tofu and cornmeal in a plastic food storage bag. Shake gently until the tofu is evenly coated.

3 Heat $1^1/_2$ tablespoons of the oil in a wide nonstick skillet. Add the tofu and sauté over medium-high heat, stirring frequently, until golden on most sides, 8 to 10 minutes. Sprinkle lightly with salt. Transfer to a container and cover to keep warm.

4 Heat the remaining tablespoon of oil in the same skillet. Add the onion and sauté over medium heat until translucent. Add the bell pepper and chile, if using, and continue to sauté until the onion and peppers are lightly browned.

5 Stir the salsa and tomatoes into the skillet and cook just until heated through, a minute or two longer.

6 To assemble, place 2 tortillas on each serving plate. Divide the salsa and onion mixture among the tortillas, then sprinkle evenly with the tofu. Sprinkle cheese over the tops, if desired, and serve at once.

Menu suggestions

> This is delicious with an easy potato dish such as Sautéed Paprika Potatoes (page 207) or Fingerling Fries (page 194). Add a simple salad of mixed greens, tomatoes, and olives.

> A colorful black bean salad is also a wonderful companion dish. Choose either Black Beans with Tomatoes, Olives, Yellow Peppers, and Croutons (page 185) or Black Bean, Mango, and Avocado Salad (page 186).

> Taco salad is a fun side dish for this meal. Mix up a bowl of dark green lettuce, diced tomatoes, bell pepper strips, olives, red or black beans, and crushed tortilla chips. Dress it any way you like.

Any-Time-of-Day Scrambled Tofu Burritos

In our home, we have lots of food rituals. This one we just call "Saturday Morning Burritos," and they are a relaxing reward for my younger son, Evan, after a busy week. Though excellent as a weekend breakfast or brunch, these are also a nice option for a quick lunch or dinner. The products I like to use for these are Nasoya firm tofu, Rudi's organic white spelt tortillas, Vegan Gourmet nacho cheese, and Muir Glen organic salsa (medium, usually cilantro-garlic). Even though Evan has had these burritos every Saturday for at least three years, he considers this meal a great gift each time I make it.

6 SERVINGS

One 16-ounce tub soft or firm (but not extra-firm) tofu
1 tablespoon nonhydrogenated margarine
1 cup salsa (your favorite variety—try black bean and corn, cilantro-garlic, chipotle, etc.)
$1/4$ to $1/2$ teaspoon curry powder
Six 8- to 10-inch soft flour tortillas
About $1^1/2$ cups grated vegan Cheddar or nacho cheese

Calories: 314
Total fat: 16 g
Protein: 11 g
Carbohydrates: 34 g
Fiber: 3 g
Sodium: 840 mg

1   Drain the tofu and cut into $1/2$-inch slices. Blot well between layers of paper towels.

2   Heat the margarine in a medium skillet. Add the tofu and mash with a potato masher or large fork.

3   Stir in the salsa and curry powder to taste, then cook over medium heat for 3 to 4 minutes, until heated through. Turn up the heat and cook a little longer if there is excess liquid that needs to evaporate.

4   Divide the scrambled tofu mixture among the tortillas, placing it in the center of each in a kind of oblong shape, and leaving room at each end. Sprinkle some cheese over the tofu (3 to 4 tablespoons for each tortilla).

5   Microwave each burrito for 30 to 40 seconds, or until the cheese is melted. Fold two ends over the tofu mixture, then roll up the rest. Repeat with each burrito, then serve at once.

Menu suggestions

See the suggestions for the previous recipe, Tofu Rancheros (page 58), which work just as well with this dish.

Tofu Aloo Gobi (Cauliflower and Potato Curry)

We've rarely gone out for Indian food without including *aloo gobi* among our selections. It's a vegetarian/vegan standard. This rendition comes together quickly, and the tofu mimics paneer, the bland, soft cheese found in some Indian dairy dishes.

1   Heat the oil in a wide skillet or stir-fry pan. Add the garlic and sauté over medium-low heat until golden.

2   Add the potatoes and about 1 cup of water. Cover and bring to a simmer, then cook over medium heat for 5 minutes.

3   Add the cauliflower, sprinkle in the ginger, garam masala, cumin, turmeric, and mustard, and continue to simmer gently for 5 minutes.

4   Stir in the tofu, tomatoes, and peas, and cook over medium-low heat for 10 minutes longer, stirring occasionally. Stir in the optional cilantro, season with salt, and serve.

Menu suggestions

> My favorite partner for this is Lentils with Greens and Sun-Dried Tomatoes (page 111). Something fruity makes a nice counterpoint to the strong flavors of the meal—a platter of orange slices with chunks of pineapple and/or mango, for example. Or, if you have more time and want to make another easy dish, try Fruitful Red Slaw (page 177).

> If you have a little more time and are accommodating larger appetites, Curried Chickpeas with Chutney Bulgur (page 98) makes a filling companion dish. Serve with a cooling salad of diced tomatoes and cucumbers (with chopped cilantro, if you'd like), dressed in a creamy vegan dressing.

6 SERVINGS

2 tablespoons olive oil

2 garlic cloves, minced

2 large potatoes, peeled and diced

1 medium head cauliflower, cut into small florets

2 teaspoons grated fresh or jarred ginger

1 teaspoon garam masala or good-quality curry powder, or more to taste

1/2 teaspoon ground cumin

1/2 teaspoon turmeric

1/2 teaspoon dry mustard

8 ounces firm or extra-firm tofu, sliced, blotted dry, and cut into small dice

2 medium or 3 plum tomatoes, diced

1/2 cup frozen green peas

1/4 cup minced fresh cilantro, optional

Salt to taste

Calories: 177
Total fat: 8 g
Protein: 10 g
Carbohydrates: 20 g
Fiber: 5 g
Sodium: 50 mg

Speedy Ways to Prepare Tofu

Sautéed Tofu: Here's a preparation I've been making for years. It's in my earlier book, *The Vegetarian 5-Ingredient Gourmet,* as an actual recipe, but it can just as easily be improvised. Slice, blot dry, and dice a 16-ounce tub of extra-firm tofu. Gently heat a tablespoon or so each of soy sauce, olive oil, and maple syrup or agave nectar in a wide skillet. Before they get too hot, add the tofu. Stir quickly to coat, then sauté over medium-high heat, stirring occasionally, until the tofu turns golden and crisp. Season with additional soy sauce to taste. If you like, add some grated ginger and/or sliced scallions to this preparation.

BBQ-Flavored Skillet Tofu: This is such a staple in my home that I can't imagine doing without it. I use two 16-ounce tubs of extra-firm tofu, sliced, blotted dry, and diced. One tub would disappear in about two seconds in my home, but for two or three people—no teenage guys among them—one 16-ounce tub may suffice. The tofu goes into a lightly oiled wide skillet or stir-fry pan with a little more natural, good-quality barbecue sauce than seems necessary. Cook over medium-high heat until some of the tofu starts to brown here and there, stirring regularly. This takes about 20 minutes, during which you can prepare a simple quinoa, pasta, or potato dish and make a simple salad.

Teriyaki Tofu Steaks: If you have a hot oven going for another dish, this is a good thing to roast at the same time if your meal needs extra protein. This is truly not a recipe, though it will seem like one when it comes out of the oven! Preheat the oven to 425°F and line a roasting pan or baking sheet with baking parchment. Cut a 16-ounce block of tofu crosswise into 6 slabs, then blot well (since I have teenage sons, I always double this). Arrange the tofu in the prepared pan. You can cut shallow diagonal slashes into the tofu so it will absorb the sauce a little more deeply. Spoon a little good-quality, natural teriyaki sauce over each slab of tofu. Bake for 10 minutes, then flip gently. Spoon a little more teriyaki over each slab of tofu, then bake for 10 to 15 minutes longer.

Cornmeal-Crusted Tofu: For a terrific tofu side dish, follow the first three steps in Tofu Rancheros (page 58) to make cornmeal-crusted tofu. Serve with salsa, teriyaki sauce, or ketchup, depending on what will work best with your meal.

Cornmeal-Crusted Seitan

If you want to dress up seitan just a bit, sautéing it until crisp with a golden cornmeal crust does the job nicely.

1 Combine the cornmeal and $^3/_4$ cup boiling water in a large heatproof mixing bowl. Let stand for 1 minute, then stir. Add the flour, optional yeast, seasoning, and salt, and whisk together.

2 Add the seitan to the bowl and stir to coat the seitan pieces evenly.

3 Heat the oil in a wide nonstick skillet. Arrange the seitan in the skillet in a single layer, if possible, or work in batches. Sauté over medium-high heat on all sides until the cornmeal turns golden brown and crusty. Serve at once.

Menu suggestions

> Like the previous recipe, this works nicely in a Parisian-style *assiette*. See the suggestions in the box on page 67; as well as the menu suggestions with Seitan and Mushrooms in Paprika Cream (page 68).

> This goes well with whole-grain dishes; here are a few ideas. With any of these, add some colorful raw vegetables or a simple salad: Quinoa with Wild Mushrooms and Mixed Squashes (page 90); Quinoa with Cauliflower, Cranberries, and Pine Nuts (page 92); Curried Cashew Couscous (page 93); or Lemony Couscous with Broccoli (page 94).

> Cornmeal-Crusted Seitan is a good partner for Sweet and White Potato Salad with Mixed Greens (page 188) or Warm Mediterranean Potato Salad (page 193). With the latter, add some grape tomatoes to the plate.

4 SERVINGS

$^1/_4$ cup yellow cornmeal, preferably stone-ground

$^1/_4$ cup whole wheat pastry flour

1 tablespoon nutritional yeast, optional

$1^1/_2$ teaspoons salt-free seasoning (such as Spike or Mrs. Dash)

$^1/_4$ teaspoon salt

Two 8-ounce packages seitan stir-fry strips or 1 pound fresh seitan, cut into thin strips

2 tablespoons olive oil, or as needed

Calories: 253
Total fat: 9 g
Carbohydrates: 13 g
Protein: 30 g
Fiber: 9 g
Sodium: 710 mg

63

Seitan and Polenta Skillet with Fresh Greens

Caravan of Dreams is one of the restaurants where my family likes to eat when we're in New York City. It's a funky, comfortable place in the East Village, with food that's hearty and innovative (and all vegan). Once, my younger son ordered the Green Garden Platter, described as "seasonal mixed greens sautéed with grilled marinated seitan, garlic, and olive oil, topped with grilled carrot polenta in mushroom gravy."

I was intrigued by the combination of seitan and polenta, so when I got home, I made my own version, which bears little resemblance to the restaurant's. There's something enticing about the seitan/polenta synergy, and with the addition of greens, the result is a great-looking, hearty dish.

4 TO 6 SERVINGS

One 18-ounce tube polenta

$1^1/2$ tablespoons olive oil

Cooking oil spray, optional

1 tablespoon reduced-sodium soy sauce

1 pound seitan, cut into bite-size pieces or strips

4 large or 6 medium stalks bok choy, with leaves, sliced crosswise

5 to 6 ounces baby spinach

4 scallions, sliced

1 tablespoon balsamic vinegar, or more to taste

$1/4$ cup oil-packed sliced sun-dried tomatoes, optional

Salt and freshly ground pepper to taste

Calories: 332
Total fat: 9 g
Protein: 34 g
Carbohydrates: 29
Fiber: 5 g
Sodium: 1170 mg

1   Cut the puckered ends off the polenta, then slice $1/2$ inch thick. Cut each slice into 4 little wedges.

2   Heat a wide nonstick skillet. Add a drop of the oil and spread it around with a paper towel to create a very light coat, or use cooking oil spray. Add the polenta wedges; cook in a single layer over medium heat until lightly browned, about 5 minutes on each side.

3   Transfer the polenta to a plate. Heat the oil and soy sauce slowly in the same skillet. Before they get too hot, add the seitan and stir well. Raise the heat to medium-high and sauté, stirring frequently, for 5 minutes. Stir in the bok choy, spinach, and scallions, then cover and cook until just wilted, 1 to 2 minutes.

4   Sprinkle in vinegar to taste. Gently fold in the polenta wedges and sun-dried tomatoes, if using. Season with salt and pepper and serve at once.

Menu suggestions

My preferred accompaniment to this family favorite is Fingerling Fries (page 194). If you can't come by fingerling potatoes, Sautéed Paprika Potatoes (page 207) works well, too. Microwaved sweet potatoes make an even easier (and more nourishing) accompaniment. Complete the meal with a simple green salad or a platter of raw veggies.

Garlicky Greens with Seitan and Soy Sausage

Tofurky sausage is a fun protein source that provides plenty of flavor and spice to a meal. I prefer it to other kinds of faux sausages because it's made with tofu and seitan rather than textured soy protein (see notes on this product in the introduction, page 19). The bold taste of Tofurky sausage provides a perfect foil for fresh greens.

4 TO 6 SERVINGS

1 1/2 tablespoons olive oil

4 to 5 garlic cloves, minced

One 8-ounce package seitan, cut into bite-size strips

One 14-ounce package Tofurky sausage, any flavor, cut into 1/2-inch slices

1 good-sized bunch Swiss chard or kale (8 to 12 ounces)

1/4 cup white wine or water

4 to 5 ounces baby spinach

Salt and freshly ground pepper to taste

Calories: 370
Total fat: 17 g
Protein: 40 g
Carbohydrates: 16 g
Fiber: 10 g
Sodium: 1030 mg

1   Heat the oil in a wide skillet or stir-fry pan. Add the garlic, seitan, and sausage and sauté over medium-low heat until the garlic is golden, stirring frequently,

2   Meanwhile, trim the stems and midribs from the greens, rinse well, and chop. Add the greens and wine to the skillet (if using kale, add water as needed to keep the skillet moist). Cover and cook 5 to 7 minutes for the chard and 10 to 12 minutes for the kale, or until the greens are cooked to your liking. Stir occasionally.

3   Add the spinach, cover, and cook briefly until wilted, then uncover and cook for another minute or so. Season with salt and pepper, then serve.

Menu suggestions

> For a supereasy way to complete the meal, serve with couscous (see Easy Ways to Dress Up Grains, page 95) or microwaved sweet potatoes. Middle Eastern Chopped Salad (page 191) synergizes nicely with this.

> Another way to round out the meal is with any simple pasta side dish (see Easy Ways to Dress Up Pasta and Noodle Side Dishes, page 121), Maple-Roasted Baby Carrots (page 205), and a platter of cherry tomatoes and sliced bell peppers.

How to Make a Parisian-Style Assiette

An *assiette* (which means plate) is a meal composed of several simply prepared, aesthetically arranged components. In the vegetarian cafés of Paris, the protein is provided by seitan, tofu, or tempeh, prepared in uncomplicated ways. My favorite kind of plate features seitan, and for a homemade version, I recommend either Seitan and Mushrooms in Paprika Cream (page 68) or Cornmeal-Crusted Seitan (page 63). Tempeh Fries with Horseradish or Wasabi-Dill Mayonnaise (page 78) or Teriyaki Tofu Steaks (page 62) are two other possibilities for the protein portion of the plate.

Assiettes often feature grated raw vegetables, usually carrots, with the addition of either turnips or beets. Grated Daikon and Carrot Salad (page 174) works well, but you can simply grate a small amount of one or more of these vegetables, either mixed together or placed in separate mounds on each plate.

There is always a cooked vegetable or two, usually something green (most often zucchini, green beans, or broccoli). Next, a timbale-shaped serving of grain, either couscous or rice or a combination of grains like quinoa and bulgur, sits in the middle of the platter. (To create a timbale, just pack cooked grain firmly into a $1/2$-cup measure and invert onto the plate.) Sometimes, a few wedges of tomato and three or four black olives adorn the plate.

Arrange all these components pleasingly on individual plates, and voilá—you've created a gorgeous *assiette* with an assortment of colors, flavors, and textures. This kind of meal might require a little more effort than many of the other express meals in this book, but not that much more. It's a lot of fun, though, and you can save it to serve on special occasions, like an intimate dinner for two (you'll likely have leftovers) or a lovely meal for two couples.

Seitan and Mushrooms in Paprika Cream

I adore Paris. When I need to assuage my longing for this lovely city, I serve my family *assiettes* (referring to a generous platter of a number of components) like those typically served in the city's vegetarian restaurants. The menus of these restaurants are not as extensive or innovative as those in the United States or Britain, but they do offer delicious, fresh food prepared with French flair. Seitan is a common offering. This one is an amalgam of seitan dishes I enjoyed at Le Potager du Marais, near the Georges Pompidou Center, and Les Cinq Saveurs D'Ananda in the Latin Quarter. For tips on creating Parisian-style *assiettes*, see the box preceding the recipe.

4 SERVINGS

1 1/2 tablespoons olive oil

2 medium onions, halved and thinly sliced

1 pound seitan, cut into bite-size pieces

8 to 10 ounces cremini or baby bella mushrooms, sliced

1/4 cup dry white or red wine

2 tablespoons unbleached white flour

1/2 cup rice milk, plus more if needed

1/2 cup plain Silk creamer

2 teaspoons sweet paprika

Salt and freshly ground pepper to taste

Calories: 313
Total fat: 11 g
Protein: 33 g
Carbohydrates: 20 g
Fiber: 4 g
Sodium: 615 mg

1   Heat the oil in a wide skillet. Add the onions and sauté over medium heat until translucent. Add the seitan and mushrooms, cover, and cook, stirring occasionally, until the onions are golden brown and the seitan is browned here and there. Pour in the wine and stir.

2   Place the flour in a small bowl. Use some of the rice milk to dissolve the flour into a smooth paste. Add the remaining rice milk, dissolved flour, and Silk creamer to the skillet and stir together. Stir in the paprika and cook over low heat for 5 minutes longer.

3   If the sauce becomes too thick, thin with a little additional rice milk. Season with salt and pepper and serve at once.

Menu suggestions

> To extend the Parisian theme, serve with Salade Janine (page 186) as a first course, then follow with the seitan dish and an easy side dish of broccoli, asparagus, or Brussels sprouts. See suggestions under My Favorite Simple Vegetable Side Dishes (page 203).

> This dish also pairs well with cooked grains of your choice (see Easy Ways to Dress Up Grains, page 95), potatoes, or sweet potatoes. A combination of sweet and white potatoes, sautéed in olive oil, is good with this. Complete the meal with a simple salad of greens and tomatoes.

Jerk-Spiced Seitan

I've always wanted a luscious, reliable (and, of course, easy) jerk seitan recipe, like the one served by my family's favorite Hudson Valley restaurant, Luna 61 in Tivoli, New York. But all the recipes I've found rely on lengthy lists of spices, Scotch bonnet peppers, and substantial time for marinating the seitan. After a couple of attempts to follow authentic recipes, with so-so results, I decided to throw authenticity to the wind and go for the flavors that I craved. This recipe may not be the genuine article, but its bold flavors never disappoint.

4 SERVINGS

Jerk sauce
1 tablespoon cornstarch
1/2 cup tropical fruit juice (mango, papaya, or pineapple)
2 tablespoons molasses or maple syrup (see Note)
2 to 3 tablespoons reduced-sodium soy sauce, to taste
1 to 2 tablespoons lime juice, to taste
1 teaspoon Jamaican jerk seasoning mix, or more to taste

2 tablespoons olive oil
1 large red or yellow onion, quartered and thinly sliced
1 medium red bell pepper, cut into long, narrow strips
1 medium green bell pepper, cut into long, narrow strips
1 pound seitan, cut into bite-size strips

Calories: 300
Total fat: 9 g
Protein: 3 g
Carbohydrates: 25 g
Fiber: 9 g
Sodium: 830 mg

1   In a small bowl, dissolve the cornstarch in 2 tablespoons or so of water. Add the remaining sauce ingredients and whisk to combine.

2   Heat 1 tablespoon of the oil in a wide skillet or stir-fry pan. Add the onion and sauté over medium-low heat until translucent. Add the peppers and continue to cook until the onions and peppers are lightly browned. Transfer to a dish.

3   Heat the remaining tablespoon of oil in the same skillet. Add the seitan and sauté over medium-high heat, stirring frequently until golden brown on most sides.

4   Pour in the sauce, reduce the heat to medium, and cook for a minute or so longer, until the sauce has thickened and the seitan is nicely glazed.

5   Stir in the onions and peppers and serve at once.

Note   Molasses adds a more assertive flavor to the sauce. I prefer molasses to maple syrup here, but it definitely makes a statement.

Menu suggestions

> For a delightful meal, serve with microwaved sweet potatoes and Creole Coleslaw (page 178) or Fruitful Red Slaw (page 177). If time allows, add Garlicky Greens (page 201).

> Serve with a hot cooked grain (see Easy Ways to Dress Up Grains, page 95) and a mixed greens salad from the Recipe Not Required choices on page 192.

> Jazz up the plate with Mixed Greens with Sprouts, Apple, and Daikon (page 179) and an easy potato dish like Fingerling Fries (page 194) or Sautéed Paprika Potatoes (page 207).

Seitan Gyros

Here is a kinder, gentler version of gyros, the Greek meat-on-a-pita classic. Seitan makes a superb stand-in, and the shortcut creamy cucumber dressing gives the entire enterprise a refreshing zip. For heartier appetites, a serving would be two gyros; one is filling enough for moderate appetites or when other dishes will be served.

4 OR 8 SERVINGS

$1^1/_2$ tablespoons olive oil

1 large onion, finely chopped

2 garlic cloves, minced

16 ounces seitan, thinly sliced

$^1/_2$ teaspoon dried oregano

$^1/_2$ teaspoon ground cumin

1 large cucumber, peeled

$^1/_3$ cup vegan ranch or creamy dill dressing, or more as needed

8 pita breads (preferably whole grain), regular or pocketless

$1^1/_2$ cups thinly shredded dark green lettuce

3 medium plum tomatoes, thinly sliced, or more as needed

PER GYRO
Calories: 311
Total fat: 5 g
Protein: 22 g
Carbohydrates: 64 g
Fiber: 7 g
Sodium: 670 mg

1   Heat the oil in a medium skillet. Add the onion and sauté over medium-low heat until translucent. Add the garlic and continue to sauté until both are just beginning to turn golden.

2   Add the seitan, oregano, and cumin. Raise the heat to medium and continue to sauté until the seitan is golden and crisp on most sides, then remove from the heat.

3   Quarter the cucumber lengthwise, cut away seeds if watery, and slice. In a small bowl, stir together the cucumber and dressing.

4   To assemble, place 1 or 2 pitas on individual serving plates. Arrange a little lettuce over each pita, followed by the seitan and the cucumber mixture. Arrange 3 slices or so of tomato down the center of each. Have everyone fold the pitas and eat out of hand.

Menu suggestions

> These are heavenly with Rosemary Roasted Potatoes with Black Olives (page 195). The gyros are also delicious with Fingerling Fries (page 194) or Sautéed Paprika Potatoes (page 207). Prepare a platter of bell peppers, baby carrots, and pickled beets to add color to the meal.

> For a lighter meal, serve with steamed broccoli (or Steamed Broccoli with Cauliflower, page 204) or green beans instead of potatoes, but do include the raw vegetable platter.

> Though I don't have a recipe for gazpacho in this book, it's easy to find one. This classic cold summer soup is a splendid companion to the gyros for a summer soup-and-sandwich meal.

Tempeh, Kale, and Sweet Potato Skillet

The first time I made this lively dish, I realized that it had elements in it that each member of my family didn't like: My husband is not crazy about tempeh, my younger son doesn't particularly like nuts in cooked dishes, my older son is not a sweet potato fan, and I'm not that big on garlic. Why would I bother with such a dish, then? Surprisingly, the unifying element is kale, something everyone in my family has grown quite fond of. Taken as a whole, this colorful and supremely nourishing dish is a big hit, with no one singling out the separate parts they don't like.

6 SERVINGS

2 medium sweet potatoes

2 tablespoons olive oil

1$\frac{1}{2}$ tablespoons reduced-sodium soy sauce

One 8-ounce package tempeh, any variety, cut into $\frac{1}{4}$-inch slices crosswise

1 good-sized bunch kale (8 to 12 ounces)

3 to 4 garlic cloves, minced

One 15- to 16-ounce can salt-free diced tomatoes

2 teaspoons good-quality curry powder, or to taste

$\frac{1}{4}$ to $\frac{1}{2}$ teaspoon Thai red curry paste, dissolved in a little warm water, optional

2 scallions, minced

$\frac{1}{2}$ cup cashew pieces

Salt and freshly ground pepper to taste

Calories: 304
Total fat: 14 g
Protein: 16 g
Carbohydrates: 31 g
Fiber: 3.5 g
Sodium: 180 mg

1   Microwave the sweet potatoes until done but still nice and firm, allowing 2 to 3 minutes per potato. Plunge into a bowl of ice water. When cool enough to handle, peel, cut in half lengthwise, and cut into thick slices.

2   Heat 1 tablespoon of the oil and the soy sauce in a stir-fry pan. Add the tempeh and stir quickly to coat. Sauté over medium heat until golden and beginning to turn crisp, 5 to 7 minutes, stirring frequently. Transfer to a plate.

3   Meanwhile, cut the leafy part of the kale away from the stems and coarsely chop into bite-size pieces. Rinse well.

4   Heat the remaining tablespoon of oil in the stir-fry pan. Add the garlic and sauté over low heat until golden.

5   Add the kale along with about $\frac{1}{2}$ cup water, the tomatoes, curry powder, and optional curry paste. Cover and cook over medium heat for 8 to 10 minutes, until the kale is tender but still bright green.

6   Stir in the scallions and cashews and cook, uncovered, for 2 to 3 minutes longer. Season with salt and pepper and serve at once.

Menu suggestions

The perfect companion for this dish is a crunchy slaw, so choose either Fruitful Red Slaw (page 177) or Creole Coleslaw (page 178). Or, you can simply combine precut coleslaw with slivered red peppers and a creamy vegan dressing. Accompany the meal with fresh pita or other fresh flatbread.

Tempeh and Green Beans with Shiitake-Miso Gravy

Slender green beans, slivered tempeh, and colorful bell pepper make for a tasty trio. The time-saver here is the use of frozen organic baby green beans, available in most any natural foods store and many supermarkets. If you have more time, do use fresh slender green beans, by all means, when they make their rare appearance at your local market.

6 SERVINGS

Shiitake-Miso Gravy (page 217)
One 8-ounce package tempeh, any variety
2 tablespoons olive oil
2 tablespoons reduced-sodium soy sauce
One 10-ounce package frozen whole baby green beans, completely thawed
One red, yellow, or orange bell pepper, cut into long, narrow strips
Toasted slivered or sliced almonds, optional

Calories: 218
Total fat: 10 g
Protein: 14 g
Carbohydrates: 18 g
Fiber: 2 g
Sodium: 555 mg

1   Prepare the gravy, cover, and set aside.

2   Cut the tempeh into $1/4$-inch-thick slices crosswise, then cut these in half lengthwise to get narrow strips.

3   Heat the oil and soy sauce slowly in a skillet, then add the tempeh strips and stir gently to coat. Sauté over medium heat for 2 to 3 minutes, stirring frequently.

4   Gently stir in the green beans and bell pepper and turn the heat to medium-high. Continue to sauté, stirring frequently, for 5 minutes longer.

5   Stir in the gravy, top with almonds if desired, and serve at once.

Menu suggestions

To make this dish, you have two recipes to follow (the dish itself and the gravy), so give yourself a break and complete the meal with no further recipes. Serve this over brown rice, quinoa, couscous, or noodles; add a platter of sliced oranges, tomatoes, and pineapple chunks.

BBQ Tempeh Bacon with Black-Eyed Peas and Greens

In this tasty "down home" dish, bits of tart apple add a delightful flavor twist. If you have the time, make a pan of your favorite vegan corn bread.

1   Heat the oil in a wide skillet. Add the onion and sauté over medium-low heat until translucent.

2   Add the garlic and tempeh bacon and sauté, stirring frequently, until everything is golden and just beginning to brown lightly.

3   Stir in the black-eyed peas, apple, and barbecue sauce. Cook over medium-high heat for 10 minutes or until the sauce is reduced.

4   Add the greens and cover until wilted. Stir the greens, then cook for another 2 minutes or so for the spinach, or 4 minutes for the chard, until tender but still bright green. Serve at once.

Variation   This is also wonderful with kale, but it needs more cooking time than chard or spinach. Start steaming it separately just before starting the dish; once cooked to your liking, stir it in at the end.

Menu suggestions

> My favorite companion for this dish is Cheese Grits with Corn (page 96). Add a simple green salad to the meal.

> Another nice way to complete this meal is with Fruitful Red Slaw (page 177) or Creole Coleslaw (page 178) and microwaved sweet potatoes.

4 TO 6 SERVINGS

2 tablespoons olive oil
1 medium onion, finely chopped
2 to 3 garlic cloves, minced
One 6-ounce package Fakin' Bacon tempeh strips, finely chopped
One 15- to 16-ounce can black-eyed peas, drained and rinsed
1 medium Granny Smith apple, diced
2/3 cup natural barbecue sauce (try smoke-flavored)
10 to 12 ounces Swiss chard or spinach, well washed, stemmed, and chopped

Calories: 325
Total fat: 11 g
Protein: 13 g
Carbohydrates: 45 g
Fiber: 9 g
Sodium: 1170 mg

Tempeh Fries with Horseradish or Wasabi-Dill Mayonnaise

If your meal needs just a little extra something in the protein department, but not necessarily a filling main dish, this is a nice choice. It also works well as an appetizer. These fries can be a bit addictive, so you may want to double the recipe if serving hungry tempeh fans.

4 SERVINGS

2 tablespoons olive oil

2 tablespoons reduced-sodium soy sauce

One 8-ounce package tempeh, any variety

Horseradish or wasabi-dill mayonnaise

1/4 cup vegan mayonnaise

2 tablespoons rice milk

1 tablespoon prepared horseradish or 1 teaspoon wasabi, or to taste

2 to 3 teaspoons lemon or lime juice

1/4 cup minced fresh dill

Calories: 278
Total fat: 16 g
Protein: 17 g
Carbohydrates: 15 g
Fiber: <1 g
Sodium: 390 mg

1   Heat the oil and soy sauce in a wide skillet. Add the tempeh, stirring quickly to coat. Sauté over medium-high heat, stirring gently and frequently, until golden and crisp, about 7 minutes.

2   Meanwhile, combine the mayonnaise, rice milk, and horseradish and lemon juice to taste in a small serving bowl and whisk until smooth. Stir in the dill.

3   When the fries are done, arrange them on a platter. Serve at once, passing around the sauce.

Menu suggestions

> This is a good addition to lighter Asian-style noodle dishes, such as Pineapple Coconut Noodles (page 114), Pad Thai (page 116), Singapore-Style Yellow Curry Rice Noodles with Tofu (page 118), Soba Noodles with Green Beans and Almonds (page 127), or Coconut-Curry Bean Thread Noodles (page 115).

> Tempeh fries are also good for boosting the protein content of meals in which salad is the main event. Try these with Warm Potato and Black Bean Salad with Red Peppers and Artichokes (page 159), Gado Gado (page 160), or Hoison-Flavored Cold Asian Noodles with Crisp Vegetables (page 168).

Barbecue-Flavored Roasted Tempeh and Vegetables

If you're looking for an undemanding tempeh dish that makes a large quantity, here's a good choice.

1 Preheat the oven to 425°F. Line a roasting pan with foil and lightly oil it.

2 Cut the tempeh in half lengthwise, then crosswise into short, $1/2$-inch-thick strips.

3 Stir all the ingredients together in a mixing bowl, then transfer to the prepared pan.

4 Bake for 20 to 25 minutes, until the vegetables are just tender, stirring after the first 10 minutes, then serve.

Menu suggestions

> Serve the meal with baked or microwaved sweet potatoes and any of the Recipe Not Required mixed greens salads on page 192.

> For a lighter accompaniment, roast some cauliflower florets, tossed in a little olive oil, at the same time as the tempeh. A salad of mixed greens from the Recipe Not Required suggestions works well with this, too.

> A light soup makes a good first course to this dish. Good choices are Asian Noodle Soup with Bok Choy and Shiitake Mushrooms (page 30) or Miso Soup with Sweet Potatoes and Watercress (page 36). Serve the tempeh dish with a platter of raw vegetables.

6 SERVINGS

Oil for the pan

Two 8-ounce packages tempeh, any variety

1 green bell pepper, cut into wide strips

1 red bell pepper, cut into wide strips

1 cup baby carrots

1 medium zucchini, sliced $1/2$ inch thick

1 medium red onion, halved and thinly sliced, rings separated

1 cup small whole baby bella or cremini mushrooms, optional

1 cup natural barbecue sauce, or as needed to coat ingredients

Calories: 324
Total fat: 9.5 g
Protein: 23 g
Carbohydrates: 36 g
Fiber: 2 g
Sodium: 330 mg

Bok Choy, Edamame, Cashew, and Orange Rice

Paella Vegetariana

Valencian Rice and Red Beans

Thai Pineapple Stir-Fried Rice

Gingery Rice with Sweet Potatoes and Peas

Quinoa with Wild Mushrooms and Mixed Squashes

Quinoa with Corn and Scallions

Quinoa with Cauliflower, Cranberries, and Pine Nuts

Curried Cashew Couscous

Lemony Couscous with Broccoli

Cheese Grits with Corn

Bulgur with Lentils, Parsley, and Raisins

Curried Chickpeas with Chutney Bulgur

Chana Masala

Polenta with Black Beans and Spinach

Black and White Beans with Citrus and Mint

BBQ-Flavored White Beans with Sausage and
    Spinach

Tortilla Casserole

Miso-Ginger Red Beans with Broccoli

Dilled Red Beans with Pickled Beets

Stewed Lentils with Soy Sausage

Lentils with Greens and Sun-Dried Tomatoes

CHAPTER THREE

Glorious Grains and Bountiful Beans

Grains and beans almost make me long for the postsixties days of vegetarianism, before soy foods, seitan, and meat substitutes of all stripes became so ubiquitous. Not to knock them, of course, but they do make it easy to forget about their extremely worthy but unglamorous cousins. I've read interviews with celebrity vegetarians or vegans in which one of the questions is, "Do you prefer tofu or tempeh?" No one is ever asked, "Do you prefer chickpeas or black beans?"

In this chapter, I focus mainly on four staple grains out of the vast array of possibilities: brown rice, bulgur, quinoa, and whole wheat couscous. Brown rice, because it's such a basic; bulgur and quinoa, because they're tasty and quick-cooking (15 to 20 minutes); and whole wheat couscous, because it's superquick to cook (5 to 10 minutes). Technically, you may know, couscous is a form of pasta, but its presentation and uses are decidedly grainlike, so it's most at home in this chapter. When you're not pressed for time, explore the world of grains beyond this quartet—barley, kasha, teff, millet, wild rice, and others.

Finally, what can I say about beans that has not already been said by philosophers, poets, nutritionists, and comedians? If I can't be original, I'll at least be brief and call for wider and more creative use of this completely uncontroversial, undisputedly delicious, and nourishing food group. This chapter can be a good starting point.

A Note About Brown Rice

In my previous book, *Vegetarian Express*, I used quick-cooking brown rice for the sake of saving time (lots of it). Truthfully, I'm not crazy about quick-cooking rice and use it only once in this chapter—in a vegan paella, in which the rice is best cooked together with the other ingredients. In other instances in this chapter, additional ingredients are prepared while the rice cooks, so once the grain is ready, there is little additional cooking time.

In the introduction, I explain that dishes made with brown rice would exceed the general goal total for the recipes in this book (to be ready in 30 minutes or less) by 10 to 15 minutes. If you don't mind quick-cooking brown rice, use it, by all means; it definitely is a time-saver. If you think of it, cook brown rice ahead of time and have it in the refrigerator, ready when you need it. And finally, if you're a pressure cooker user, there's your solution.

When I call for brown rice, feel free to substitute its more exotic varieties—jasmine, basmati, black forbidden, and others. They all take about the same amount of time to cook—30 to 35 minutes—and add a little something special to your meals.

Bok Choy, Edamame, Cashew, and Orange Rice

This bountiful rice dish offers a variety of flavors and textures. I especially like the burst of sweetness provided by tiny orange sections.

1 Combine the rice and 3$\frac{1}{2}$ cups water in a medium saucepan. Bring to a boil, then lower the heat. Cover and simmer gently until the water is absorbed, 30 to 35 minutes.

2 A few minutes before the rice is done, heat the oil in a stir-fry pan. Add the edamame and bell pepper and stir-fry over medium-high heat for 2 to 3 minutes. Add the bok choy and scallions and continue to stir-fry for 1 to 2 minutes, just until wilted.

3 Stir in the cooked rice and sesame oil, mixing well. Season to taste with teriyaki sauce, ginger, and pepper. Stir in the orange sections and cashews and serve at once.

Menu suggestions

Since this dish involves an abundance of diverse ingredients, I like to complete the meal with few additional recipes. Sautéed Tofu (page 62) can be prepared while the rice is cooking. A platter of grape tomatoes and baby carrots round out the meal nicely. If you want to add one more item, steamed broccoli would be just the thing. Or, if time is not an issue, may I suggest upgrading that to Spicy Sesame Broccoli (page 197)?

4 TO 6 SERVINGS

1$\frac{1}{2}$ cups long-grain brown rice, rinsed

1 tablespoon light olive oil

1 cup frozen edamame (fresh green soybeans), completely thawed

1 medium red or orange bell pepper, cut into short, narrow strips

6 stalks bok choy, sliced thinly on the diagonal (leaves included)

3 to 4 scallions, thinly sliced

1 teaspoon dark sesame oil

2 to 4 tablespoons good-quality teriyaki or reduced-sodium soy sauce

1 to 2 teaspoons grated fresh or jarred ginger

Freshly ground pepper

2 small oranges, such as clementines, peeled and sectioned

$\frac{1}{2}$ cup toasted cashew pieces

Calories: 289
Total fat: 5 g
Protein: 9 g
Carbohydrates: 54 g
Fiber: 5 g
Sodium: 200 mg

Paella Vegetariana

This is an easy dish to make, and the results are splendid. Using quick-cooking rice, you can have a magnificent one-dish meal in about thirty minutes, whether for a busy weeknight or a leisurely weekend meal.

6 SERVINGS

2 tablespoons extra virgin olive oil

1 medium onion, chopped

2 to 3 garlic cloves, minced

1 green bell pepper, cut into 2-inch strips

1 red bell pepper, cut into 2-inch strips

2 cups diced tomatoes

One 15-ounce can vegetable broth

One 6-serving package quick-cooking brown rice

1 teaspoon saffron threads, dissolved in a small amount of hot water (see Note)

½ teaspoon dried thyme

One 14-ounce can artichoke hearts, drained and coarsely chopped

1½ cups frozen green peas, thawed

¼ cup chopped fresh parsley

Salt and freshly ground pepper to taste

Calories: 293
Total fat: 9 g
Protein: 9 g
Carbohydrates: 48 g
Fiber: 6.5 g
Sodium: 665 mg

1   Heat the oil in a Dutch oven or stir-fry pan. Add the onion and garlic and sauté over medium heat until translucent, about 5 minutes.

2   Add the green pepper and half of the red pepper (set aside the rest for garnish) and sauté for 5 minutes, stirring frequently.

3   Add the tomatoes, broth, rice, saffron, thyme, and 1 cup water. Bring to a simmer, then cover and simmer gently for 10 minutes.

4   Stir in the artichoke hearts, peas, and half of the parsley. Check to see if the rice is completely done. Add a small amount of water to cook further if necessary or to add a bit more moisture to the mixture. Season with salt and pepper. Cook just until everything is heated through, about 3 minutes.

5   Transfer the rice mixture to a large, shallow serving dish or serve straight from the pan. Garnish with a concentric circle of the reserved red pepper strips and sprinkle the remaining parsley over the top. Serve at once.

Note   Substitute 1 teaspoon turmeric if saffron is unavailable.

Menu suggestions

> Chickpea and Carrot Salad with Parsley and Olives (page
> 190) is a fantastic companion dish. If time allows, add
> steamed asparagus, green beans, or Brussels sprouts to the
> meal.

> Spinach and Red Cabbage Salad with Oranges and Almonds
> (page 180) also teams well with this recipe, as do many of
> the suggestions for mixed greens salads under Recipe Not
> Required (page 192 the ones containing fruits and nut. As
> with the previous menu suggestion, a steamed green
> vegetable is a good addition if you have a bit more time.

Valencian Rice and Red Beans

A classic Spanish dish, this is a great choice when you want something easy and hearty. Briny olives perk up the mellow flavor of brown rice and beans.

6 SERVINGS

1¼ cups long-grain brown rice, rinsed

2 tablespoons extra virgin olive oil

1 large onion, quartered and thinly sliced

4 garlic cloves, minced

1 green bell pepper, diced

One 16-ounce can small red beans, drained and rinsed

1½ cups diced tomatoes

⅔ cup pimiento-stuffed green olives, sliced

3 scallions, thinly sliced

1 teaspoon dried oregano

¼ teaspoon dried thyme

Cayenne or dried red pepper flakes

Salt and freshly ground pepper to taste

¼ to ½ cup chopped fresh cilantro or parsley to taste

Calories: 293
Total fat: 9 g
Protein: 9 g
Carbohydrates: 48 g
Fiber: 6.5 g
Sodium: 665 mg

1   Combine the rice with 3 cups water in a small saucepan and bring to a rapid simmer. Lower the heat, cover, and simmer until the water is absorbed, 30 to 35 minutes. If you like a more tender grain, add another ½ cup water and cook until absorbed.

2   About 15 minutes before the rice is done, heat the oil in a wide skillet. Add the onion and sauté over medium-low heat until translucent. Add the garlic and bell pepper and sauté until all are golden.

3   When the rice is done, add it to the skillet along with the beans, tomatoes, olives, scallions, oregano, thyme, and cayenne to taste. Cook for 5 minutes, or until everything is heated through. Season with salt and pepper, then stir in cilantro to taste. Serve at once.

Menu suggestions

> Complete this meal with a salad of mixed greens with seedless orange sections and toasted sliced or slivered almonds, dressed in a natural vinaigrette or olive oil and balsamic vinegar. On the side, serve Zucchini and Summer Squash Sauté (page 209) or steamed broccoli.

> Polenta slices grilled on a very lightly oiled pan go well with this, as do steamed cauliflower florets. If time allows, make both; if not, choose one. Complete the meal with a platter of red and yellow peppers, artichoke hearts, cherry tomatoes, and orange slices.

Thai Pineapple Stir-Fried Rice

Colorful and luscious, this Thai restaurant classic can easily be made at home.

1   Combine the rice with 3 cups water in a saucepan. Bring to a rapid simmer, then cover and simmer gently until the water is absorbed, 30 to 35 minutes.

2   Shortly before the rice is done, heat the oil in a stir-fry pan or extra-wide skillet. Add the onion and sauté over medium heat until golden.

3   Add the broccoli, carrots, and bell pepper. Turn the heat to medium-high and stir-fry for 3 minutes or so, just until the vegetables are tender-crisp.

4   Add the scallions, tomatoes, and pineapple chunks and continue to stir-fry for a minute or two, just until the tomatoes soften slightly.

5   Stir in the cooked rice, then add the coconut milk, soy sauce, curry powder, and ginger. Stir gently until all the ingredients are completely combined. Serve at once, passing around chopped cashews to top individual servings, if desired.

Menu suggestions

This is one of those dishes with so much going for it that you can complete the meal with no further recipes. Serve with a platter of sliced Thai-flavored baked tofu and one of the mixed greens salads under Recipe Not Required (page 192). I especially like this with the one that contains sliced pickled beets, cucumbers, and daikon radish.

6 SERVINGS

$1^1/_2$ cups long-grain brown rice, rinsed
$1^1/_2$ tablespoons olive oil
1 medium onion, quartered and sliced
2 cups small broccoli florets
2 medium carrots, sliced
1 medium red or orange bell pepper, diced
3 to 4 scallions, sliced
2 medium tomatoes, diced
One 16-ounce can unsweetened pineapple chunks, drained
1 cup light coconut milk
2 tablespoons reduced-sodium soy sauce
1 teaspoon curry powder
2 teaspoons minced fresh or jarred ginger
Chopped cashews, optional

Calories: 315
Total fat: 7.5 g
Protein: 6 g
Carbohydrates: 59 g
Fiber: 5 g
Sodium: 205 mg

Gingery Rice with Sweet Potatoes and Peas

In the classic Thai dish, white rice is combined with white potatoes. Though it sounds rather redundant, the seasonings and embellishments make it delectable nonetheless. I took the general idea of this recipe and revved it up to include the two main ingredients' more nourishing counterparts—brown rice and sweet potatoes. This may still sound like an odd combination, but honestly, it works very well. Like any dish using brown rice, this will take about forty minutes, but hands-on time is limited, allowing you to prepare any accompaniments at a leisurely pace.

6 SERVINGS

1½ cups long-grain brown rice, rinsed
2 medium sweet potatoes
2 tablespoons light olive oil
6 scallions, sliced
3 to 4 garlic cloves, minced
2 teaspoons minced fresh or jarred
    ginger, or to taste
1 teaspoon good-quality curry powder
½ teaspoon turmeric
1 cup frozen green peas, thawed
Salt to taste
¼ cup minced fresh cilantro, or more
    to taste
Chopped peanuts or cashews, optional

Calories: 278 g
Total fat: 6 g
Protein: 6 g
Carbohydrates: 51 g
Fiber: 4 g
Sodium: 45 g

1   Combine the rice with 3½ cups water in a small saucepan. Bring to a rapid simmer, then lower the heat. Cover and simmer gently until the water is absorbed, 30 to 35 minutes.

2   Meanwhile, microwave the sweet potatoes until just done but still nice and firm. Start with 3 minutes total, then test. A knife should go through with some resistance. If needed, microwave for another minute at a time. Once done, plunge the sweet potatoes into a bowl of cold water. Set aside until needed.

3   When the rice is nearly done, peel the sweet potatoes and cut them into ½-inch dice.

4   Heat the oil in a stir-fry pan. Add the white parts of the scallions and the garlic, and sauté over medium-low heat until just turning golden. Add the scallion greens and the sweet potatoes; turn the heat to medium-high and stir-fry for a minute or so.

5   Stir in the ginger, curry powder, and turmeric, then add the rice. Turn the heat to medium-high and cook, stirring, until the ingredients are well blended. Add the peas and cook, stirring frequently, for 3 to 4 minutes.

6 Season with salt, stir in the cilantro, and serve. Top each serving with some chopped nuts if desired.

Menu suggestions

> Serve with a platter of baby corn, sliced tomatoes, half-sour pickles, and sliced baked or smoked tofu. Complete the meal with steamed broccoli or Spicy Sesame Broccoli (page 197).

> If you have time to make a companion dish, I recommend Tempeh Fries with Horseradish or Wasabi-Dill Mayonnaise (page 78). Embellish the plate with sliced tomatoes, baby carrots, and bell peppers.

Quinoa with Wild Mushrooms and Mixed Squashes

Earthy and hearty, this kind of grain and mushroom dish appeals to me most in the fall, though it can be served any time of year.

1 cup quinoa, rinsed in a fine sieve

1 natural, salt-free vegetable bouillon cube

1 tablespoon olive oil

1 medium onion, chopped

2 garlic cloves, minced

1/4 cup dry white wine or water

1 medium zucchini, halved lengthwise and sliced

1 medium yellow summer squash, halved lengthwise and sliced

6 to 8 ounces cremini or baby bella mushrooms, sliced

1/4 cup chopped fresh parsley or cilantro, or more to taste

1/2 teaspoon dried oregano, or more to taste

1/2 teaspoon ground cumin, or more to taste

Salt and freshly ground pepper to taste

Calories: 251
Total fat: 6 g
Protein: 9 g
Carbohydrates: 39 g
Fiber: 5 g
Sodium: 200 mg

1   Combine the quinoa and bouillon cube with 2 cups water in a medium saucepan and bring to a simmer. Cover and simmer gently until the water is absorbed, about 15 minutes.

2   Heat the oil in a skillet or stir-fry pan. Add the onion and garlic and sauté over medium heat until translucent.

3   Add the wine, if using, the squashes, and mushrooms, and sauté over medium-high heat until the squashes are touched with golden spots.

4   Stir in the cooked quinoa, followed by the parsley, oregano, and cumin. Cook over low heat, stirring frequently, for 3 to 5 minutes longer. Season with salt and pepper, then serve at once.

Menu suggestions

> Salads with a little sweetness provide a nice balance to this dish. Try Mixed Greens with Sprouts, Apple, and Daikon (page 179), Fruitful Red Slaw (page 177), or Spinach and Red Cabbage Salad with Oranges and Almonds (page 180). To boost the protein content of the meal, serve with Garlic and Lemon Beans (page 110).

> You can also complete this meal simply with sautéed vegan sausage links (my favorite, as I've mentioned several times, is Tofurky brand) and a salad of greens and tomatoes.

Quinoa with Corn and Scallions

What's not to love about quinoa? It's a powerhouse of nutrients, it cooks in fifteen minutes, and its pleasantly offbeat flavor is most appealing. I try to use it often, and this quick preparation is the one I turn to the most. If you have time, use lightly cooked fresh corn kernels (from three medium ears) instead of frozen.

1   Combine the quinoa and bouillon cube with 2$\frac{1}{2}$ cups water in a medium saucepan and bring to a simmer. Cover and simmer gently for 10 minutes.

2   Stir in the corn, scallions, and cumin, and continue to cook, still covered, until the water is absorbed and the quinoa is puffy, about 5 minutes longer.

3   Remove from the heat and stir in the fresh herb and oil. Season with salt and pepper, then serve.

Menu suggestions

> This is companionable with several of the legume dishes in this chapter, including Stewed Lentils with Soy Sausage (page 108), Lentils with Greens and Dried Tomatoes (page 111), and Dilled Red Beans with Pickled Beets (page 107). Add a platter of raw vegetables or a green salad.

> Tempeh dishes that go well with this include Tempeh and Green Beans with Shiitake-Miso Gravy (page 76) and Barbecue-Flavored Roasted Tempeh and Vegetables (page 79). As with the previous suggestion, a green salad or a platter of raw vegetables completes the meal.

6 SERVINGS

1$\frac{1}{4}$ cups quinoa, rinsed in a fine sieve

1 natural, salt-free vegetable bouillon cube

2 cups frozen corn kernels, thawed

3 to 4 scallions, sliced

1 teaspoon ground cumin

$\frac{1}{4}$ cup minced fresh herb of your choice (cilantro, parsley, or dill, or a combination), or more to taste

2 tablespoons flaxseed or extra virgin olive oil

Salt and freshly ground pepper to taste

Calories: 227
Total fat: 7.5 g
Protein: 7 g
Carbohydrates: 36 g
Fiber: 4 g
Sodium: 35 mg

Quinoa with Cauliflower, Cranberries, and Pine Nuts

If I had to choose a favorite quinoa dish, it would be this one. With just a few ingredients, it manages to showcase sweet, savory, and nutty flavors all at once.

4 TO 6 SERVINGS

1¼ cups quinoa, rinsed in a fine sieve

2 tablespoons fragrant oil, such as walnut or untoasted sesame (if unavailable, use olive oil)

1 medium yellow or red onion, finely chopped

1 small head cauliflower, cut into small pieces and florets

½ cup dried cranberries

⅓ cup pine nuts, lightly toasted in a dry skillet

¼ cup minced fresh parsley, or more to taste

Salt and freshly ground pepper to taste

Calories: 416
Total fat: 16 g
Protein: 13 g
Carbohydrates: 59 g
Fiber: 8 g
Sodium: 60 mg

1   Combine the quinoa with 2½ cups water in a saucepan and bring to a simmer. Cover and simmer gently for 15 minutes, or until the water is absorbed.

2   Meanwhile, heat 1 tablespoon of the oil in a wide skillet or stir-fry pan. Add the onion and sauté over medium-low heat until golden. Add the cauliflower and about ⅓ cup water. Cover and cook for 5 minutes, or until the cauliflower is just tender.

3   Once the quinoa is done, add it to the cauliflower mixture, followed by the cranberries, pine nuts, and parsley. Toss together, then remove from the heat. Drizzle in the remaining oil and season with salt and pepper. Serve at once.

Menu suggestions

> Team this lively grain dish with Black Beans with Tomatoes, Olives, Yellow Peppers, and Croutons (page 185) and steamed green beans, Brussels sprouts, or asparagus.

> Another delightful companion is Lentils with Greens and Sun-Dried Tomatoes (page 111). Add a simple salad of greens and tomatoes to this meal.

> The quinoa is a nice complement to any easy tofu dish, such as Sautéed Tofu or BBQ-Flavored Skillet Tofu (both on page 62), along with any colorful salad.

Curried Cashew Couscous

Here's a delicious, substantial grain dish that's ready in minutes, leaving you plenty of time to build a meal around it.

1   Combine the couscous with 2 cups water and the bouillon cube in a wide skillet or stir-fry pan. Bring to a simmer, then cover and let stand off the heat for 5 to 10 minutes, or until the water is absorbed.

2   Add the remaining ingredients, stir together well, then cook, stirring frequently, for 2 to 3 minutes longer. Transfer to a serving bowl, and serve at once.

Menu suggestions

>   An Indian-style legume or vegetable dish goes well with this easy grain preparation. Just ahead in this chapter, you'll find Chana Masala (page 99), a curried chickpea dish. Add a salad of diced tomatoes and cucumbers (with chopped fresh dill or cilantro, if you'd like) in a creamy vegan dressing, and pass around some chutney (store-bought or Apricot Chutney, page 225).

>   This also teams well with earthy lentil dishes like Stewed Lentils with Soy Sausage (page 108) or Lentils with Greens and Sun-Dried Tomatoes (page 111). The tomato and cucumber salad described above will complement this meal as well.

>   See the menu with Black and White Beans with Citrus and Mint (page 102).

4 TO 6 SERVINGS

1 cup couscous, preferably whole wheat

1 natural, salt-free vegetable bouillon cube

1 cup frozen green peas, thawed

2 tablespoons fragrant nut oil (such as walnut) or flaxseed oil

1/2 cup chopped cashews

1 teaspoon good-quality curry powder, or more to taste

1 teaspoon grated fresh or jarred ginger, or more to taste

1/2 teaspoon turmeric

1/2 cup raisins, dried cherries, or dried cranberries

2 scallions, thinly sliced

Salt and freshly ground pepper to taste

Calories: 414
Total fat: 16 g
Protein: 11 g
Carbohydrates: 59 g
Fiber: 6 g
Sodium: 90 mg

Lemony Couscous with Broccoli

This may be too light to serve as a meal's centerpiece, but it's perfect for pairing with a dish of equal heft, like a bean or legume dish or a main dish salad. I've also enjoyed leftovers of this served cold in a wrap with shredded lettuce and sliced tomatoes.

6 SERVINGS

3/4 cup couscous, preferably whole wheat

2 tablespoons extra virgin olive oil

1 medium red onion, quartered and thinly sliced

3 cups finely chopped broccoli florets

1/4 cup minced fresh parsley

2 tablespoons minced fresh dill

Juice of 1 lemon

1/3 cup oil-packed sliced sun-dried tomatoes or chopped pitted black olives, preferably oil-cured

Calories: 170
Total fat: 7 g
Protein: 5 g
Carbohydrates: 24 g
Fiber: 3 g
Sodium: 50 mg

1   Combine the couscous with 1 1/2 cups boiling water in a heatproof container. Cover and let stand for 10 minutes, then fluff with a fork.

2   Meanwhile, heat 1 tablespoon of the oil in a large skillet. Add the onion and sauté over medium heat until golden.

3   Add the broccoli and just enough water to keep the bottom of the skillet moist, then cover and allow to steam until the broccoli is bright green and tender-crisp, about 4 minutes.

4   Add the couscous to the skillet along with the parsley and dill, lemon juice, and sun-dried tomatoes. Stir together well, cook for 2 or 3 minutes longer, then serve.

Menu suggestions

> When a meal's centerpiece is a main dish salad but you want a little more substance, this is a good addition. Spinach, Artichoke, and Chickpea Salad (page 156) and Asian Edamame and Tofu Chopped Salad (page 158) are good choices.

> Some companionable pairings with legume dishes from this chapter include Stewed Lentils with Soy Sausage (page 108), Lentils with Greens and Sun-Dried Tomatoes (page 111), BBQ-Flavored White Beans with Sausage and Spinach (page 102), and Miso-Ginger Red Beans with Broccoli (page 106). Complete these meals with a simple salad.

Easy Ways to Dress Up Grains

In this book, I most often suggest brown rice, quinoa, or couscous when a grain side dish enhances a meal. There's nothing wrong with serving these grains plain, but with minimal extra effort, you can tease out a more interesting effect. Here are a few ways to do so:

• Before cooking, toast the grains for five minutes or so on a dry skillet to bring out their nutty flavor and aroma.

• Toss in a natural, salt-free bouillon cube for extra flavor as the grains cook. When done, stir in a little nonhydrogenated margarine or, better yet, flaxseed or nut oil.

• Stir in some fresh herbs (parsley, dill, mint, or cilantro).

• Add some chopped scallions and a dash each of dark sesame oil and soy sauce.

• Stir in some salsa and chopped cilantro.

• Pass around some good-quality teriyaki sauce to top the grains.

Cheese Grits with Corn

Here's a tasty and speedy side dish my family loves. It's a good accompaniment to bean dishes, and is a nice change of pace from potatoes or rice.

4 TO 6 SERVINGS

1 cup quick-cooking grits, preferably stone-ground

1½ cups frozen corn kernels, thawed

1½ tablespoons nonhydrogenated margarine

1 cup grated vegan Cheddar or nacho cheese

Salt to taste

Calories: 318
Total fat: 13 g
Protein: 6.5 g
Carbohydrates: 46 g
Fiber: 5 g
Sodium: 235 mg

1   Bring 4 cups water to a gentle simmer in a medium saucepan. Slowly whisk in the grits, stirring constantly to avoid lumps. Cook gently over low heat for 5 minutes, or until tender and thick.

2   Stir in the corn, margarine, and cheese. Cook for another minute or two, until the cheese is fairly well melted.

3   Season with salt and serve.

Menu suggestions

> This dish definitely invites a southern theme. My favorite way to serve it is with BBQ Tempeh Bacon with Black-Eyed Peas and Greens (page 77), microwaved sweet potatoes, and any kind of coleslaw you like. This can be as basic as combining precut coleslaw cabbage with vegan ranch dressing or vegan mayonnaise, but if you have the inclination to make one more recipe for this meal, choose from Creole Coleslaw (page 178) or Fruitful Red Slaw (page 177).

> For an even easier meal, pair this with Garlic and Lemon Beans (page 110)—using black beans is an especially nice option with this meal. Add steamed broccoli and a platter of cherry tomatoes, baby carrots, peppers, and olives.

Bulgur with Lentils, Parsley, and Raisins

This is inspired by *mujaddarah,* a traditional Middle Eastern dish that is sometimes made with rice, and sometimes with cracked wheat. The grain is combined with lentils and lots of onions browned in olive oil. Even in its basic form, it's delicious. Since we save some time by cooking (rather than soaking) the bulgur, I like to dress up this classic with the nontraditional but tasty additions of scallions and raisins.

1   Combine the bulgur and bouillon cube with 2 cups water in a small saucepan. Bring to a rapid simmer, then cover and cook for 15 minutes, or until the water is absorbed.

2   Meanwhile, heat the oil in a wide skillet. Add the onion and sauté over medium-low heat until lightly browned, stirring frequently, about 15 minutes. Stir in the lentils and cook just until heated through.

3   Combine the bulgur and onion-lentil mixture in a serving dish and stir in all the remaining ingredients. Serve at once.

Menu suggestions

> A fun and flavorful meal: Serve this with Sweet and White Potato Salad with Mixed Greens (page 188), homemade or store-bought hummus, oil-cured olives, and fresh pita bread.

> For another meal with a Middle Eastern theme, team this with Middle Eastern Chopped Salad (page 191), homemade or store-bought hummus, stuffed grape leaves, and fresh pita bread.

6 SERVINGS

1 cup bulgur

1 natural, salt-free vegetable bouillon cube

2 tablespoons extra virgin olive oil

1 large onion, finely chopped

One 15-ounce can brown lentils, drained and rinsed

3/4 cup finely chopped fresh parsley

2 scallions, thinly sliced

1/2 cup dark or golden raisins

1 teaspoon ground cumin, or more to taste

Salt and freshly ground pepper to taste

Calories: 230
Total fat: 5.5 g
Protein: 8.5 g
Carbohydrates: 39 g
Fiber: 10 g
Sodium: 115 mg

GLORIOUS GRAINS AND BOUNTIFUL BEANS

VEGAN EXPRESS

Curried Chickpeas with Chutney Bulgur

Curry-scented chickpeas perch prettily atop a bed of chutney-flavored bulgur, making for a highly appealing grain and legume combination.

SERVES 6

1¼ cups bulgur

One 15- to 16-ounce can chickpeas, drained and rinsed

3 medium tomatoes, diced

2 teaspoons good-quality curry powder, or to taste

½ teaspoon ground cumin

¼ teaspoon turmeric

2 to 3 scallions, thinly sliced

¼ cup minced fresh cilantro, plus more for topping if desired

1 tablespoon nonhydrogenated margarine

One 8- to 9-ounce jar sweet and spicy chutney (such as mango)

Salt to taste

Calories: 242
Total fat: 4 g
Protein: 7 g
Carbohydrates: 47 g
Fiber: 10 g
Sodium: 340 mg

1   Combine the bulgur with 2½ cups water in a small saucepan. Bring to a rapid simmer, then cover and simmer gently for 15 minutes, or until the water is absorbed.

2   Meanwhile, combine the chickpeas, tomatoes, curry powder, cumin, and turmeric in a small saucepan. Bring to a simmer, then simmer gently for 5 minutes. Cover until needed.

3   When the bulgur is done, stir in the scallions, cilantro, margarine, and chutney. Season with a little salt. To serve, mound a portion of the bulgur on each plate and top with a portion of the chickpea mixture. Garnish with additional cilantro, if desired.

Variation   Make this with whole wheat couscous in place of bulgur. Combine 1¼ cups couscous with 2½ cups water in a heatproof container; let stand for 5 to 10 minutes, until the water is absorbed, then fluff with a fork.

Menu suggestions

> Serve this with steamed broccoli or green beans along with a simple salad of crisp cucumbers dressed in a creamy vegan dressing. Add fresh flatbread, if you'd like.

> For a colorful meal, combine this with Cauliflower and Carrot Salad (page 189) and microwaved sweet potatoes.

Chana Masala

This simplified version of an Indian favorite is a delightful way to showcase tasty chickpeas.

1   Heat the oil in a wide skillet. Add the onion and sauté until translucent. Add the garlic and continue to sauté until the onion is golden.

2   Add the chickpeas, garam masala, turmeric, ginger, tomatoes, lemon juice, and about $1/4$ cup water. Bring to a simmer, then cook over medium-low heat for 10 minutes, stirring frequently. This should be moist and stewlike, but not soupy; add a little more water, if needed.

3   Stir in the cilantro and season with salt. Serve on its own in shallow bowls or over a hot cooked grain, if desired.

Menu suggestions

> Omit the option of a plain cooked grain; see the menu with Curried Cashew Couscous (page 93).

> If you choose to serve this with a plain cooked grain, as suggested in the recipe, complete the meal with fresh flatbread and Fruitful Red Slaw (page 177).

> If time allows, make Apricot Chutney (page 225) as an accompaniment with any menu.

4 SERVINGS

1 tablespoon olive oil
1 large onion, chopped
2 to 3 garlic cloves, minced
Two 15- to 16-ounce cans chickpeas, drained and rinsed
1 to 2 teaspoons garam masala or good-quality curry powder
$1/2$ teaspoon turmeric
2 teaspoons grated fresh or jarred ginger
2 large tomatoes, diced
1 tablespoon lemon juice
$1/4$ cup minced fresh cilantro, or to taste
Salt to taste
Hot cooked grain (rice, quinoa, or couscous), optional

Calories: 320
Total fat: 6 g
Protein: 12 g
Carbohydrates: 56 g
Fiber: 6 g
Sodium: 645 mg

Polenta with Black Beans and Spinach

Prepared polenta provides an easy way to add variety to the dinner repertoire. I often use it sliced and sautéed as a side dish, but occasionally, it will become an intrinsic part of a recipe, as it is here.

4 SERVINGS

Two 18-ounce tubes polenta
Olive oil cooking spray
1 tablespoon extra virgin olive oil
2 to 3 garlic cloves, minced
One 15- to 16-ounce can black beans, drained and rinsed
1/4 cup sliced oil-packed sun-dried tomatoes
1 teaspoon ground cumin
5 to 6 ounces baby spinach
Freshly ground pepper

Calories: 339
Total fat: 6 g
Protein: 13 g
Carbohydrates: 58 g
Fiber: 10.5 g
Sodium: 1210 mg

1   Cut the puckered ends off each tube of polenta, then cut each tube into 12 slices about $1/2$ inch thick. Heat a wide nonstick griddle that has been generously sprayed with olive oil cooking spray. Arrange the polenta slices on the griddle. Cook both sides over medium-high heat until golden and crisp, about 8 minutes per side.

2   Meanwhile, heat the olive oil in a wide skillet or stir-fry pan. Add the garlic and sauté over low heat for a minute or so, just until golden.

3   Add the beans, sun-dried tomatoes, and cumin. Stir together and cook over medium heat just until heated through.

4   Add the spinach, cover, and cook just until it wilts, 1 to 2 minutes. Stir the mixture together, season with pepper to taste, and remove from the heat.

5   To serve, arrange 3 or 4 polenta slices on each plate and spoon the bean mixture evenly over each serving.

Menu suggestions

> This is delicious accompanied by Sautéed Paprika Potatoes (page 207). Add Mixed Greens with Sprouts, Apple, and Daikon (page 179) or the Recipe Not Required green salad containing pickled beets, sliced crisp cucumber, and daikon radish or turnip (page 192).

> Serve this with a light, easy pasta dish. The first three possibilities under Easy Ways to Dress Up Pasta and Noodle Side Dishes (page 121) are all good ones; or combine cooked pasta with your favorite natural marinara sauce. Add a simple green salad to this meal.

Black and White Beans with Citrus and Mint

Juicy orange sections and mint add a surprising twist to this hearty dish of black and white beans.

6 SERVINGS

1½ tablespoons olive oil

1 medium red onion, quartered and thinly sliced

½ orange or red bell pepper, finely diced

One 15- to 16-ounce can black beans, drained and rinsed

One 15- to 16-ounce can navy beans, drained and rinsed

2 to 3 scallions, thinly sliced

¼ cup orange juice, preferably fresh

2 clementines or other small, seedless oranges, peeled and sectioned

1 teaspoon grated orange zest, optional

Thinly sliced mint leaves

Salt and freshly ground pepper to taste

Calories: 192
Total fat: 4 g
Protein: 9.5 g
Carbohydrates: 30 g
Fiber: 4 g
Sodium: 220 mg

1　Heat the oil in a wide skillet or stir-fry pan. Add the onion and sauté over medium heat until translucent. Add the bell pepper and continue to sauté until the onion is golden.

2　Add both kinds of beans, the scallions, and orange juice, and cook over medium heat until hot, 3 to 4 minutes.

3　Stir in the clementines, optional zest, and mint as desired. Season with salt and pepper and serve.

Menu suggestions

> In season, serve with steamed asparagus or Sautéed Asparagus with Almonds (page 203); otherwise, pair with steamed broccoli or Brussels sprouts. Add simply embellished grains on the side (see Easy Ways to Dress Up Grains, page 95), and a platter of sliced bell peppers, tomatoes, and cucumbers.

> Pair this with either of the couscous dishes in this chapter—Curried Cashew Couscous (page 93) or Lemony Couscous with Broccoli (page 94). Round out the meal with a basic salad of mixed greens or dark green lettuce, tomatoes, peppers, and cucumbers.

BBQ-Flavored White Beans with Sausage and Spinach

I fully admit that this recipe screams "emergency dinner!" But it's spicy, hearty, high in protein, and best of all, ready for the table in about twenty minutes. Some nights, you need a main dish like that, and this one never disappoints.

1   Heat the oil in a wide skillet or stir-fry pan. Add the onion and sauté over medium heat until translucent.

2   Add the garlic and sausage; continue to sauté, stirring frequently, until everything is golden, about 5 minutes.

3   Stir in the beans and barbecue sauce. Cook until piping hot, about 4 minutes.

4   Add the spinach and cover. When it wilts down a bit, stir it in. Continue to cook for just a minute or so longer. Serve at once.

Menu suggestions

> A salad with a hint of sweetness balances the hearty, bold flavors in this dish. Choose Fruitful Red Slaw (page 177) or Creole Coleslaw (page 178). To make the meal even heartier, add some cooked quinoa or microwaved sweet potatoes.

> If this is truly an emergency meal, stick with the basics— microwaved Yukon gold or sweet potatoes and a simple green salad.

6 TO 8 SERVINGS

1¹/₂ tablespoons olive oil
1 medium onion, chopped
2 garlic cloves, minced, optional
One 14-ounce package Tofurky sausage, sliced ¹/₂ inch thick
Two 15- to 16-ounce cans navy beans, drained and rinsed
1 cup natural barbecue sauce, any flavor
4 to 5 ounces baby spinach

Calories: 380
Total fat: 13 g
Protein: 25 g
Carbohydrates: 44 g
Fiber: 13 g
Sodium: 790 mg

Tortilla Casserole

Here's my favorite recipe from this book's predecessor, *Vegetarian Express,* now out of print. I just had to bring it forward to this book; it's one of those dishes that saves the day when you're low on fresh groceries, since it's made largely of pantry and freezer staples. It's also a reliable dish for feeding last-minute company. In this slightly updated version, I've added homemade vegan sour cream (which is entirely optional, but adds a big "yum" factor to the dish) and a variation of an added vegetable layer.

6 SERVINGS

One 15- to 16-ounce can pinto, pink, or
  black beans, drained and rinsed
One 15- to 16-ounce can crushed
  tomatoes
One 4-ounce can chopped mild green
  chiles
2 cups frozen corn kernels, thawed
2 scallions, minced
1/2 teaspoon ground cumin
1/2 teaspoon dried oregano
Oil for the dish
10 corn tortillas
1 1/2 cups grated vegan Monterey Jack,
  Cheddar or nacho cheese
Steamed vegetables, optional (see
  Variation)
Salsa (red or green)
Vegan Sour Cream (page 213),
  optional

Calories: 295
Total fat: 10 g
Protein: 9 g
Carbohydrates: 45 g
Fiber: 9 g
Sodium: 315 mg

1   Preheat the oven to 400°F.

2   Combine the beans, tomatoes, chiles, corn, scallions, cumin, and oregano in a mixing bowl. Mix thoroughly.

3   Lightly oil a wide, shallow 2-quart rectangular or round casserole and layer as follows: 5 tortillas, overlapping one another; half of the bean mixture; half of the cheese; and the optional vegetable layer. Repeat the tortilla, bean, and cheese layers.

4   Bake the casserole for 12 to 15 minutes, or until the cheese is bubbly. Let stand for a minute or two, then cut into squares or wedges to serve. Pass the salsa and optional sour cream for topping.

Variation   For the optional vegetable layer, use either 10 to 12 ounces lightly steamed and well-drained baby spinach or lightly sautéed thin slices of zucchini and/or yellow summer squash; you'll need two medium squashes for this.

Menu suggestions

> If you're not making the optional squash layer in the casserole, Zucchini and Summer Squash Sauté (page 209) is a good side dish with this meal. If you want the meal to be more substantial, cook some quinoa while the casserole is in the oven. Add some curly lettuce and cherry or grape tomatoes to garnish the plate.

> Serve with microwaved white or sweet potatoes and Creole Coleslaw (page 178). Or, to keep this meal as easy as possible, serve with a simple green salad rather than the slaw.

Miso-Ginger Red Beans with Broccoli

It's unusual to give a bean dish an Asian spin, but the balance of colors, textures, and flavors in this dish work very well indeed. Its flavors are modeled on those used with adzuki beans, small red beans used in Japanese cuisine.

4 TO 6 SERVINGS

1½ tablespoons light olive oil

1 large onion, quartered and thinly sliced

2 garlic cloves, minced

4 cups bite-size broccoli florets

2 large tomatoes, diced

Two 15- to 16-ounce cans small red beans

2 teaspoons grated fresh or jarred ginger, or more to taste

2 to 3 tablespoons dark miso

1½ tablespoons cornstarch

2 teaspoons dark sesame oil

Hot cooked grain (rice, couscous, or quinoa)

Calories: 300
Total fat: 8.5 g
Protein: 17 g
Carbohydrates: 50 g
Fiber: 14 g
Sodium: 630 mg

1   Heat the oil in a large skillet; sauté the onion over medium heat until golden. Add the garlic and broccoli; sauté, covered, until the broccoli is bright green, 2 to 3 minutes.

2   Add the tomatoes, beans, and ginger. Simmer over low heat for 10 minutes.

3   In a small bowl, combine the miso, cornstarch, and 1 cup warm water; whisk together until smooth. Add to the skillet along with the sesame oil. Simmer gently until the liquid has thickened. Serve at once over or alongside the hot cooked grain.

Menu suggestions

> Not only does Great Grated Veggies with Tahini Dressing (page 175) pair beautifully with this, it allows you to use up the broccoli stems as well. Grated Daikon and Carrot Salad (page 174) is an equally good partner, and simpler than the former to make. I like to add sliced tomatoes or pickled beets to the plate for extra color.

> Two more colorful salad choices for this meal are Spinach and Red Cabbage Salad with Oranges and Almonds (page 180) or Tri-Color Sweet and Tangy Peppers (page 181).

Dilled Red Beans with Pickled Beets

This colorful, subtly sweet-sour bean dish provides a nice contrast to mild pasta, potato, or grain dishes.

1   Heat the oil in a medium skillet. Add the onion and sauté over medium heat until limp.

2   Add the cabbage and continue to sauté until the vegetables are golden.

3   Stir in the beans, beets, agave nectar, vinegar, and dill. Continue to cook over medium heat just until everything is heated through, 4 to 5 minutes. Season with salt and pepper and serve.

Menu suggestions

> Serve with Sautéed Paprika Potatoes (page 207) and one of the mixed greens salads from the Recipe Not Required suggestions (page 192).

> For a hearty meal, Creamy Pasta with Asparagus and Peas (page 128) makes a good companion dish. Add a simple salad or one of the mixed greens salads from the Recipe Not Required suggestions (page 192).

> This goes well with Quinoa Tabouleh with Pine Nuts (page 183) and corn on the cob for a tasty summer meal.

6 SERVINGS

1¹/₂ tablespoons olive oil

¹/₂ medium red onion, quartered and thinly sliced

1 cup thinly sliced green cabbage or precut coleslaw

One 28-ounce can red beans, drained and rinsed

One 12-ounce jar sliced pickled beets, drained

1 tablespoon agave nectar or maple syrup

1 tablespoon red wine vinegar, or more to taste

¹/₄ cup minced fresh dill

Salt and freshly ground pepper to taste

Calories: 153
Total fat: 3.5 g
Protein: 5.5 g
Carbohydrates: 29 g
Fiber: 6 g
Sodium: 285 mg

Stewed Lentils with Soy Sausage

Spicy Tofurky sausages make a bold statement in this easy lentil stew. If you can find beluga lentils, use them—they give this dish extra visual appeal.

4 TO 6 SERVINGS

2 tablespoons olive oil

1 medium onion, finely chopped

3 to 4 garlic cloves, minced

2 medium celery stalks, thinly sliced

One 14-ounce package Tofurky sausage, sliced $1/4$ inch thick

Two 15- to 16-ounce cans lentils, drained lightly but not rinsed

1 cup diced tomatoes

$1/2$ teaspoon dried thyme

$1/4$ cup minced fresh parsley, or more to taste

Salt and freshly ground pepper to taste

Calories: 490
Total fat: 19 g
Protein: 40 g
Carbohydrates: 45 g
Fiber: 24 g
Sodium: 925 mg

1   Heat the oil in a wide skillet. Add the onion and sauté over medium-low heat until translucent.

2   Add the garlic, celery, and sausage. Sauté, stirring frequently, until all the ingredients are golden and touched here and there with browned spots.

3   Add the lentils, tomatoes, and thyme. Turn the heat to medium-high and bring to a gentle simmer. Return to medium-low heat and cook for 3 to 4 minutes, until the tomatoes have just softened.

4   Stir in the parsley, season with salt and pepper, and serve at once in shallow bowls.

Menu suggestions

> Make a hearty meal with an easy potato dish like Fingerling Fries (page 194) or Sautéed Paprika Potatoes (page 207). Add an interesting salad chosen from the mixed greens salad suggestions under Recipe Not Required (page 192).

> If time allows, cook some brown rice and serve this dish over it on a plate rather than in shallow bowls. If you like the idea of serving this with a grain but don't want to wait for brown rice, couscous works well, too. Maple-Roasted Baby Carrots (page 205) made with the stovetop option makes a good side dish. Add a simple green salad to the meal.

> If you want a meal with no additional recipes to follow, all you need are microwaved sweet potatoes and a green salad.

A Super Side Dish: Garlic and Lemon Beans

If a meal I'm making needs a little protein boost, I must admit that the first thing I think of reaching for is tofu. But since we already use plenty of soy foods, I try to remind myself to consider beans instead. Beans of all kinds are inexpensive and delicious nutritional powerhouses—in short, a food category that deserves daily attention.

To make this basic flavorful side dish, drain and rinse one or two 15- to 16-ounce cans of black, red, or pinto beans. Heat a little extra virgin olive oil in a skillet; add 2 to 4 cloves minced garlic (depending on whether you use one or two cans, and on how much you like garlic—feel free to use as much as you like). Sauté over low heat until the garlic begins to turn golden, then add the beans and $1/4$ to $1/2$ cup water (again, depending on the amount of beans). Bring to a simmer. With a potato masher, crush just enough of the beans to thicken the base. Add lemon juice to your liking, season with pepper, and serve. You can also add a small amount of chopped parsley or cilantro to this dish.

Lentils with Greens and Sun-Dried Tomatoes

Since my family loves lentils, I keep a few cans of organic canned lentils on hand to use when we want a meal with this nourishing legume in a hurry. To make this dish a little fancier, try using beluga lentils, as I've recommended in earlier recipes. These diminutive, gleaming black lentils contrast attractively with the spinach and dried tomatoes.

1   Rinse the spinach. Place in a medium skillet with just enough water to keep the bottom moist. Cover and steam until just wilted, 1 to 2 minutes. Remove from the heat, drain in a colander, and press out excess liquid.

2   Combine the the remaining ingredients in a medium saucepan and stir together over medium heat. When hot, stir in the spinach. Check the seasoning and serve.

Menu suggestions

I've recommended this as a speedy companion dish several times in this chapter. See the menus with Quinoa with Cauliflower, Cranberries, and Pine Nuts (page 92), Curried Cashew Couscous (page 93), and Lemony Couscous with Broccoli (page 94). With any of these choices, complete the meal with a salad of your choice from the Recipe Not Required suggestions on page 192.

4 SERVINGS AS A SIDE DISH

8 to 10 ounces baby spinach

Two 15-ounce cans lentils, drained and rinsed (use beluga lentils, if available)

$2/3$ cup sliced oil-packed sun-dried tomatoes, with about 2 tablespoons of their oil

2 tablespoons lemon juice, or to taste

Pinch of ground cumin

$1/2$ cup minced fresh dill or parsley, or more to taste

Salt and freshly ground pepper to taste

Calories: 193
Total fat: 10 g
Protein: 8.5 g
Carbohydrates: 20 g
Fiber: 9.5 g
Sodium: 205 mg

CHAPTER FOUR

Pasta and Noodles, East to West

Pasta and noodles are probably staples in nearly everyone's kitchen: quick and easy to prepare, nourishing, and an excellent value for their modest cost. But the number one reason for their endurance and popularity, I believe, is their amazing versatility. Forgetting for a moment that Italian pastas come in hundreds of shapes, the number of dishes that can be made using long, spaghetti-like pastas alone is mindboggling. Many of us remember them as a favorite comfort food from childhood. But just as we've all grown up, so have long noodles. These days, thanks to the burgeoning popularity of ethnic cuisines, the variety available in supermarkets and natural food stores is downright dizzying. Not long ago, soba, udon, and bean thread noodles and rice vermicelli, among others, were rare finds. Now, many well-stocked supermarkets carry them.

This wide availability and versatility can be used to full advantage when creating express meals. Few carb-based foods are such welcoming vehicles for fresh vegetables and delicious sauces. If your pantry is stocked with a good variety of pastas and noodles, and your fridge is filled with the fresh ingredients that enhance them, pasta heaven is a mere thirty minutes away.

Pineapple Coconut Noodles

This dish has proven a big hit in my home. You can get all the ingredients in the Asian foods section of any well-stocked supermarket or natural foods store.

6 SERVINGS

12 ounces Asian noodles (see Note)
1 tablespoon light olive oil
4 to 6 garlic cloves, minced
One 14- to 15-ounce can light coconut milk
One 20-ounce can crushed pineapple, lightly drained
1/2 teaspoon Thai red or green curry paste, or to taste, dissolved in a little warm water
1 stalk lemongrass, cut into thirds and bruised with a knife, optional
Juice of 1/2 to 1 lime
2 tablespoons natural granulated sugar
1 teaspoon salt
6 to 8 scallions, sliced
1/4 to 1/2 cup minced fresh cilantro
Peanut halves or crushed peanuts

Calories: 308
Total fat: 9 g
Protein: 9 g
Carbohydrates: 52 g
Fiber: 4 g
Sodium: 510 mg

1 Cook the noodles in plenty of rapidly simmering water until al dente, then drain.

2 Meanwhile, heat the oil in a stir-fry pan. Add the garlic and sauté over low heat until golden. Add the coconut milk and pineapple, then whisk in the curry paste. Add the lemongrass, lime juice to taste, sugar, and salt.

3 Add the cooked noodles to the coconut mixture, along with half the scallions and cilantro to taste. Remove from the heat. If you'd like a spicier dish, stir in small amounts of additional curry paste (dissolved in a little water) until the effect is as spicy as you'd like. Serve at once, passing around the remaining scallions and the peanuts for topping.

Note This is most authentic with wide flat rice noodles, but no matter how carefully I cook them, they fall apart in the dish. Instead, I use whole-grain soba noodles. Any long, thin noodle will work, though, and this is also good with whole wheat spaghettini.

Menu suggestions

Pair this easy recipe with a basic protein dish. Good choices are BBQ-Flavored Skillet Tofu (page 62), Cornmeal-Crusted Seitan (page 63), and Tempeh Fries with Horseradish or Wasabi-Dill Mayonnaise (page 78). Add a platter of grape or cherry tomatoes, sliced bell peppers, baby corn, and carrots.

Coconut-Curry Bean Thread Noodles

Don't be daunted by the list of ingredients used here; it all comes together quickly, as the idea is to cook everything as briefly as possible. Enveloped in plenty of coconut milk, this dish of noodles and vegetables becomes quite luscious.

1   Cover the noodles with boiling water in a heatproof container. Cover and let stand for 6 to 8 minutes, or according to package directions, until al dente. Drain, rinse briefly with cool water, then use kitchen shears or a sharp knife to cut here and there into shorter lengths.

2   While the noodles are soaking, heat the oil in a stir-fry pan. Add the garlic and sauté over medium-low heat until golden.

3   Add the remaining ingredients except salt; bring to a rapid simmer, then lower the heat and simmer gently for 3 minutes.

4   Add the cooked noodles and season with salt. Cover and let stand for 5 minutes, until the noodles have absorbed much of the coconut milk, then serve.

Menu suggestions

Prepare Sautéed Tofu (page 62) or simply serve with a platter of sliced Thai-flavored baked tofu. Complete the meal with Spinach and Red Cabbage Salad with Oranges and Almonds (page 180) or Mixed Greens with Sprouts, Apple, and Daikon (page 179).

4 TO 6 SERVINGS

4 ounces bean thread (cellophane) noodles

1 tablespoon olive oil

3 garlic cloves, sliced

One 14- to 15-ounce can light coconut milk

One 15-ounce can baby corn

1 cup snow peas

1 medium zucchini, cut into eighths lengthwise, then into 2-inch strips

1 medium red bell pepper, cut into narrow 2-inch strips

1 cup sliced mushrooms, optional

3 scallions, cut into 1-inch lengths

2 teaspoons good-quality curry powder

1/4 teaspoon Thai red curry paste, or more to taste, dissolved in a little hot water

Salt to taste

Calories: 220
Total fat: 10 g
Protein: 2 g
Carbohydrates: 33 g
Fiber: 4 g
Sodium: 310 mg

Pad Thai

Here is a pleasing variation on this popular Thai noodle dish. Though the dish is more than fine without it, do try to use fresh lemongrass if possible, as it adds a subtle flavor and scent. Many supermarkets now carry this once-exotic item. But don't worry if you can't find it; I've made the recipe with and without, and it's good either way.

4 TO 6 SERVINGS

Sauce
1 cup light coconut milk
1/4 cup ketchup
2 tablespoons natural granulated
    sugar
2 tablespoons lime juice, or to taste
3 tablespoons reduced-sodium soy
    sauce

12 ounces Asian noodles (see Note)
1 1/2 tablespoons peanut or olive oil
2 to 3 garlic cloves, minced
2 cups small broccoli florets
1 stalk lemongrass, cut into thirds and
    bruised, optional
4 to 6 scallions, thinly sliced
1 cup fresh mung bean sprouts,
    optional
Dried red pepper flakes
1/4 to 1/2 cup chopped fresh cilantro
1/4 to 1/2 cup chopped roasted peanuts

Calories: 517
Total fat: 16.5 g
Protein: 17.5 g
Carbohydrates: 80 g
Fiber: 7 g
Sodium: 725 mg

1   Combine the ingredients for the sauce in a small bowl and set aside until needed.

2   Cook the noodles in plenty of rapidly simmering water until al dente, then drain.

3   While the noodles are cooking, heat the oil in a wok or stir-fry pan. Add the garlic and sauté over low heat for a minute or so, then add the broccoli lemongrass, if using, and white parts of the scallions. Add a small amount of water, raise the heat to medium, and cover. Steam for 3 to 4 minutes, or until the broccoli is tender-crisp.

4   Add the noodles, sauce, and green parts of the scallions; stir gently but thoroughly. Add just enough red pepper flakes to give the dish the kind of kick you like. Stir in cilantro and peanuts to taste and serve at once.

Note   This dish is traditionally made with wide rice noodles; however, no matter how hard I try to prevent it, this kind of noodle falls apart in the dish. There must be some secret to keeping these noodles together that I am not privy to. Instead, I use udon or somen noodles. Wide Chinese wheat noodles would work well, too.

Menu suggestions

There is no better pairing for this than Thai Tossed Salad (page 184). Since making Pad Thai is very hands-on, prepare the salad before starting the noodle dish. Otherwise, prepare a platter of raw vegetables if you don't have time to make a companion dish. If you'd like to add extra protein to the meal, serve with sliced Thai-style baked tofu.

Singapore-Style Yellow Curry Rice Noodles with Tofu

Characteristic of some Southeast Asian cuisines is the overlapping of Asian and Indian influences. This is true of this pleasantly offbeat noodle dish, which is seasoned with both soy sauce and curry.

4 SERVINGS

One 16-ounce tub firm or extra-firm tofu

Sauce
1/4 cup reduced-sodium soy sauce
1 teaspoon natural granulated sugar
1 to 2 teaspoons good-quality curry powder
1 to 2 teaspoons grated fresh or jarred ginger
1/4 cup vegetable stock, dry white wine, or water

8 ounces rice-stick noodles
1 tablespoon olive oil
1 teaspoon dark sesame oil
1 large onion, quartered and thinly sliced
2 garlic cloves, minced
1 large carrot, cut into thick 2-inch-long sticks
1 red bell pepper, cut into narrow 2-inch-long strips
1 green bell pepper, cut to match red pepper
1 cup frozen green peas, thawed

Calories: 490
Total fat: 15 g
Protein: 27 g
Carbohydrates: 66 g
Fiber: 7 g
Sodium: 625 mg

1   Cut the tofu into 1/4-inch-thick slices. Blot well between clean tea towels or several layers of paper towels. Cut into narrow strips and set aside.

2   Combine the ingredients for the sauce in a small bowl, stir together, and set aside until needed.

3   In a large saucepan or heatproof dish, cover the rice noodles with very hot water. Cover the dish and let the noodles soak for 15 to 20 minutes or until al dente, then drain. Cut the noodles in several directions to shorten (kitchen shears work well for this).

4   Meanwhile, heat the olive and sesame oils in a stir-fry pan. Add the onion, garlic, and carrot and stir-fry over medium-high heat for 4 minutes. Add the bell peppers and tofu strips and stir-fry 3 to 4 minutes longer.

5   Add the cooked noodles to the pan along with the peas and sauce. Toss quickly and stir-fry just until everything is heated through. Serve at once.

Menu suggestions

This is a quick but very hands-on dish, so I suggest simple, recipe-free accompaniments. Steamed broccoli or corn on the cob is good with this. Choose one of the suggestions for mixed greens salads under Recipe Not Required (page 192).

Vietnamese-Style Bean Thread Noodles

A pleasing composition using a minimum of exotic ingredients, this traditional Asian dish becomes somewhat offbeat through the use of fresh tomatoes and basil.

1   Cover the noodles with boiling water in a heatproof container. Cover and let stand for 6 to 8 minutes, or according to package directions, until al dente. Drain the noodles, place them on a cutting board, and chop in several directions to shorten.

2   Meanwhile, heat the oil in a wok or stir-fry pan. Add the onion and stir-fry over medium heat until translucent.

3   Turn up the heat, add the garlic and cabbage, and stir-fry until the cabbage is tender-crisp and lightly browned, 5 to 7 minutes.

4   Add the tomatoes and sprouts and continue to fry, stirring frequently, until the tomatoes are soft and the sprouts tender-crisp, another 5 to 7 minutes.

5   Stir in the vinegar, soy sauce, and red pepper flakes to taste, the sugar, tofu, and noodles. Cook, stirring, until everything is heated through. Serve at once, garnishing each serving with some chopped peanuts and basil.

Menu suggestions

This is delicious with Bok Choy, Red Cabbage, and Carrot Salad (page 176) or Thai Tossed Salad (page 184). To boost the protein content of the meal, serve slices of baked tofu at room temperature.

4 SERVINGS

4 ounces bean thread (cellophane) noodles
2 tablespoons olive or peanut oil
1 large onion, quartered and thinly sliced
2 garlic cloves, minced
2 heaping cups thinly shredded Napa or savoy cabbage
2 heaping cups diced tomatoes
1 cup fresh mung bean sprouts
2 to 3 tablespoons rice vinegar
2 to 3 tablespoons reduced-sodium soy sauce
Dried red pepper flakes
1 teaspoon natural granulated sugar
1/3 cup chopped peanuts or cashews
Thinly sliced fresh basil leaves

Calories: 294
Total fat: 13 g
Protein: 6 g
Carbohydrates: 41 g
Fiber: 4.5 g
Sodium: 295 mg

Seitan Chow Fun

Chow fun is indeed fun chow when you're in the mood for tasty Asian-style fare.

4 SERVINGS

Sauce

1$\frac{1}{2}$ tablespoons cornstarch
1 cup vegetable broth or water
2 teaspoons dark sesame oil
2 tablespoons reduced-sodium soy
    sauce
1 to 2 teaspoons grated fresh or jarred
    ginger

One 8-ounce package wide Asian
    wheat noodles or udon noodles
1$\frac{1}{2}$ tablespoons light olive oil
1 medium onion, quartered and thinly
    sliced
2 garlic cloves, minced
3 cups bite-size broccoli florets
1 medium red bell pepper, cut into
    narrow strips
One 8-ounce package seitan, cut into
    bite-size shreds
1 cup mung bean sprouts
Freshly ground pepper

Calories: 410
Total fat: 11 g
Protein: 26 g
Carbohydrates: 54 g
Fiber: 7 g
Sodium: 735 mg

1 In a small mixing bowl, dissolve the cornstarch in $\frac{1}{4}$ cup of the broth. Stir in the sesame oil, soy sauce, ginger to taste, and remaining broth. Set aside.

2 Bring a large pot of water to a boil. Cook the noodles until al dente according to package directions, then drain.

3 Heat the oil in a stir-fry pan. Add the onion and sauté over medium heat until golden. Add the garlic and broccoli and stir-fry over medium-high heat just until the broccoli begins to turn bright green. Add a small amount of water if more moisture is needed in the pan.

4 Add the bell pepper and seitan and continue to stir-fry just until the vegetables are tender-crisp, about 3 minutes longer.

5 Stir in the sprouts and sauce and cook briefly until the sauce thickens.

6 Stir in the cooked noodles and remove from the heat. Season with pepper to taste and a bit more soy sauce if desired, and serve at once.

Menu suggestions

Bok Choy, Red Cabbage, and Carrot Salad (page 176) is a nice way to add color and texture to the plate. Complete the meal with store-bought vegan spring rolls.

Nearly Instant Thai Coconut Corn Soup, page 26

Seitan and Polenta Skillet with Fresh Greens,
page 64

Thai Pineapple Stir-Fried Rice,
page 87

Pasta with Roasted Vegetables
and Olives, page 124

Sausage, Pepper, Broccoli, and Zucchini Pizza, page 144

Black Beans with Tomatoes, Olives, Yellow Peppers,
and Croutons, page 185

Berry-Apple Skillet Crumble,
page 230

Our Favorite Chocolate Cake,
page 236

Easy Ways to Dress Up Pasta and Noodle Side Dishes

Sometimes, I like to serve pasta or noodles as a side dish, rather than as the focus of a meal. For four to six people, 8 ounces of pasta is more than sufficient as a side dish. We're used to getting huge heaps of pasta when ordering it in restaurants, but at home, there's nothing wrong with a little moderation, especially if there are lots of other good things on the plate. Below, when I refer to Asian noodles, assume that this includes soba, udon, and Chinese wheat noodles, unless otherwise noted. Here are some simple ways to dress up pasta and Asian-style noodles.

Pasta Aglia Olio: Sauté lots of chopped garlic (6 to 8 cloves, or even more if you're a garlic fan) in about 1/4 cup extra virgin olive oil until golden. Combine with cooked angel hair or spaghettini (whole grain, if you'd like) in a serving bowl; stir in chopped parsley or basil as desired, then season with salt and pepper.

Mushroom Paprika Pasta: Cook a batch of presliced brown mushrooms with a tiny bit of olive oil in a covered skillet. Shortly, there will be sufficient liquid in the skillet to keep it moist. Combine the mushrooms with cooked pasta—any short, chunky shape. Drizzle in a little more olive oil, if you'd like. Season with salt and pepper and sprinkle with paprika.

Pasta with Fresh and Dried Tomatoes and Basil: Combine cooked pasta (any short chunky shape) with as many diced, flavorful fresh tomatoes as you like, along with generous amounts of sun-dried tomatoes and sliced basil leaves. Drizzle in a little extra virgin olive oil, season with salt and pepper, and serve warm or at room temperature.

Sesame-Soy Asian Noodles: Season cooked Asian noodles with soy sauce, dark sesame oil, and sesame seeds to your liking. If desired, add thinly sliced scallions as well. Another variation on this is to make Sesame-Ginger Salad Dressing (page 222) or simply use a prepared version.

Hoisin-Ginger Noodles: Hoisin sauce has a pretty intense flavor, so add sparingly to Asian noodles until the flavor is to your liking. Stir in a teaspoon or two of grated fresh or jarred ginger. This is tasty with a small amount of minced cilantro as well.

Peanut Satay Noodles: Add an 8-ounce jar of Thai peanut satay sauce to 8 ounces cooked Asian noodles. Embellish with sliced scallions and/or minced cilantro and, if desired, some chopped nuts.

Ravioli with Stir-Fried Vegetables

Here's an offbeat way to present a stir-fry. Tofu-filled ravioli are like little dumplings in this dish. Do try to use hoisin sauce to finish the dish. It creates a nice brown glaze and adds just the right flavor kick to the mild ravioli.

4 TO 6 SERVINGS

Sauce
1½ tablespoons cornstarch
2 tablespoons reduced-sodium soy sauce
1 to 2 teaspoons minced fresh or jarred ginger, to taste
2 teaspoons lime juice
2 teaspoons natural granulated sugar

One 13-ounce package frozen tofu-filled ravioli
¾ cup frozen edamame
2 tablespoons olive oil
2 garlic cloves, minced
1 long Japanese eggplant or 2 tiny eggplants
3 cups bite-size broccoli florets
1 cup slender baby carrots
8 to 10 ounces cremini or baby bella mushrooms or 4 ounces shiitakes, stemmed and sliced
¼ cup hoisin sauce, or additional soy sauce to taste

Calories: 435
Total fat: 14 g
Protein: 22 g
Carbohydrates: 62 g
Fiber: 9 g
Sodium: 710 mg

1   In a large measuring cup or small mixing bowl, dissolve the cornstarch in a little water, then add enough water to make 1 cup. Add the remaining sauce ingredients, stir together, and set aside.

2   Bring water to a boil in a large saucepan or small soup pot. Stir in the ravioli and edamame and simmer steadily for 6 to 8 minutes, or until just tender. Drain.

3   Meanwhile, heat the oil in a large stir-fry pan. Add the garlic and sauté over low heat until golden.

4   In the following order, layer the eggplant, broccoli, carrots, and mushrooms in the pan. Pour in about ½ cup water. Cover and steam for 5 minutes, then lift the lid and stir. Continue to cook, uncovered, until the vegetables are tender-crisp, 3 to 4 minutes longer.

5   Gently stir in the ravioli and edamame, followed by the sauce. Cook for a minute or so longer, until the sauce has thickened. Season with hoisin sauce or additional soy sauce and serve at once.

Menu suggestions

Serve with Spinach and Red Cabbage Salad with Oranges and Almonds (page 180). Or you might explore the possibilities for Recipe Not Required mixed greens salads (page 192).

Pasta Jambalaya

Here's one of my favorite uses for a terrific product, Tofurky sausage. The bold flavor is used to full advantage in this hearty Creole-flavored pasta dish. If you have more time, make a pan of vegan corn bread, it's a wonderful addition to this meal.

1   Cook the pasta in plenty of rapidly simmering water until al dente, then drain.

2   Meanwhile, heat the oil in a large skillet or stir-fry pan. Add the onion and sauté over medium heat until translucent. Add the garlic, celery, bell pepper, and sausage; continue to sauté until all the vegetables are lightly browned.

3   Add the tomatoes, basil, paprika, thyme, and cayenne to taste. Bring to a simmer, then cover and simmer gently for 10 minutes.

4   Stir in the pasta and parsley. Season with salt, then taste to adjust the other seasonings to your liking. Serve at once.

Menu suggestions

Creole Coleslaw (page 178) is a fitting companion, though any mixed green salad is welcome as well. See the ideas under Recipe Not Required (page 192). If time allows, add more green to the plate with steamed broccoli or green beans.

6 TO 8 SERVINGS

8 to 10 ounces chunky pasta (such as penne, cavatappi, or gemelli, whole wheat if desired)
2 tablespoons extra virgin olive oil
1 large onion, chopped
3 to 4 garlic cloves, minced
2 celery stalks, diced
1 medium green bell pepper, diced
One 14-ounce package Tofurky Italian- or kielbasa-style sausage, sliced 1/2 inch thick
One 28-ounce can diced tomatoes, with juice
1 teaspoon dried basil
1 teaspoon paprika
1/2 teaspoon dried thyme
Cayenne
1/4 cup minced fresh parsley
Salt to taste

Calories: 396
Total fat: 14 g
Protein: 26 g
Carbohydrates: 51 g
Fiber: 12 g
Sodium: 635 mg

Pasta with Roasted Vegetables and Olives

The time for this recipe may stretch to forty minutes or so, due to preheating the oven and roasting the vegetables, but it's one of my favorites, and I think it's worth that tiny bit of extra time. I hope you will, too.

6 SERVINGS

Oil for the pan

1 long, narrow Japanese eggplant, cut into 1/4-inch-thick slices (see Note)

1 large red bell pepper, cut into 1-inch squares

2 tablespoons extra virgin olive oil

4 cups small broccoli florets (or one 16-ounce bag precut florets)

1/2 medium red onion, thinly sliced

4 garlic cloves, sliced

8 to 10 ounces penne or spirals, preferably whole wheat or spelt

1/3 cup oil-packed sliced sun-dried tomatoes, plus 2 tablespoons of their oil, reserved separately

1/2 cup pitted kalamata olives

1/4 cup finely minced fresh parsley

1 tablespoon balsamic vinegar, or more to taste, optional

Dried red pepper flakes

Salt and freshly ground pepper to taste

Calories: 310
Total fat: 13 g
Protein: 9 g
Carbohydrates: 43 g
Fiber: 8 g
Sodium: 300 mg

1 Heat the oven to 425°F. Lightly oil the bottom of a large roasting pan. Bring a large pot of water to a boil.

2 Combine the eggplant and bell pepper in a mixing bowl. Drizzle with a tablespoon of the oil, then stir together and transfer to the roasting pan.

3 Combine the broccoli, onion, and garlic in the same mixing bowl and drizzle with the remaining tablespoon of oil. Transfer to the roasting pan and gently mix with the other vegetables, then place in the oven.

4 Roast the vegetables for 20 to 25 minutes, stirring every few minutes, until nicely but not overly browned. Remove from the oven, then transfer the vegetable mixture to a large pasta bowl.

5 While the vegetables are roasting, cook the pasta in plenty of rapid simmering water until al dente, then drain.

6 Add the sun-dried tomatoes, olives, parsley, and balsamic vinegar, if using, to the vegetables and mix well.

7 Add the cooked pasta to the vegetable mixture and toss together with the reserved tomato oil. Season with red pepper to taste, salt, and black pepper. Serve at once.

Note You can substitute 1 small eggplant, quartered lengthwise and sliced $\frac{1}{4}$ inch thick, for the Japanese eggplant.

Menu suggestions

Make a salad of mixed greens, tomatoes, red beans or chickpeas, pickled beets, and sliced carrots. Serve with Salsa and Olive Oil Salad Dressing (page 223). Complete the meal with a crusty whole-grain bread.

Pasta Twists with Cauliflower and Spinach

One evening not long ago, I had about one hour to make dinner for the family—and eat—between getting home from one activity and going out to another. I improvised based on what was in the fridge rather than following a recipe. This was the result; everyone liked this simple dish so much that I was compelled to compose a recipe for it, and have followed it many times since.

6 SERVINGS

10 to 12 ounces cavatappi or fusilli

2 tablespoons extra virgin olive oil

2 garlic cloves, minced

1 small head cauliflower, cut into small bite-size pieces

4 to 5 ounces baby spinach

1/4 cup oil-packed sliced sun-dried tomatoes

1/2 cup raisins

2 to 3 tablespoons minced fresh parsley

Salt and freshly ground pepper to taste

Calories: 288
Total fat: 7 g
Protein: 10 g
Carbohydrates: 52 g
Fiber: 7 g
Sodium: 70 mg

1 Cook the pasta in plenty of rapidly simmering water until al dente, then drain.

2 Meanwhile, heat 1 tablespoon of the oil in a large skillet or stir-fry pan. Add the garlic and sauté over low heat until golden.

3 Add the cauliflower and about 1/2 cup water. Cover and steam, stirring occasionally, until the cauliflower is tender but still firm, 5 to 7 minutes.

4 Layer the spinach over the cauliflower and cover. Cook for just a minute or two, until wilted, then stir into the cauliflower.

5 Add the sun-dried tomatoes, raisins, parsley to taste, pasta, and the remaining tablespoon of olive oil. Stir together gently, then season with salt and pepper and serve.

Menu suggestions

> A lively legume dish is a nice way to complete this meal. Try it with Stewed Lentils with Soy Sausage (page 108) and a salad of mixed greens and tomatoes.

> A bean salad makes for a good pairing. Black Beans with Tomatoes, Olives, Yellow Peppers, and Croutons (page 185) is delicious with this.

Soba Noodles with Green Beans and Almonds

One of my favorite things about Paris—after the museums, the streetscapes, the Seine, the style, the beauty, and so on—is the green beans. Yes, you read that right. Parisian green beans are ubiquitous, and always served perfectly ripe and tender-crisp. Here at home, perfect green beans seem to be available only for a month or so in the summer. This dish is a nice way to highlight them during that brief window; however, I'm so fond of it that I use frozen green beans so I can make this regularly. I highly recommend using organic whole baby green beans, if you can find them; otherwise, French-cut beans will do.

1   Toast the almonds in a dry skillet until golden, stirring frequently. Transfer to a plate.

2   Bring water to a boil in a large saucepan or small soup pot. Add the noodles; cook for 2 minutes, then add the green beans. Simmer steadily until the noodles are al dente and the green beans tender-crisp, 3 to 5 minutes longer, then drain.

3   Meanwhile, combine the hoisin sauce and soy sauce to taste, the agave nectar, and vinegar in a small bowl and stir together.

4   Combine the noodles and sauce in a serving dish. Add the scallions and toss. Season with pepper to taste, toss again, and serve.

Menu suggestions

> This teams nicely with Spicy Sesame Broccoli (page 196). Add a platter of raw vegetables and strips of baked tofu.

> Salads that pair well with this are Great Grated Veggies with Tahini Dressing (page 175), Bok Choy, Red Cabbage, and Carrot Salad (page 176), and Spinach and Red Cabbage Salad with Oranges and Almonds (180). With any of these choices, you can also add a platter of baked tofu.

---

4 TO 6 SERVINGS

1/3 cup sliced almonds
8 ounces soba noodles
One 10-ounce bag frozen whole baby green beans or French-cut green beans
2 to 3 tablespoons hoisin sauce
1 tablespoon reduced-sodium soy sauce, or to taste
1 tablespoon agave nectar or maple syrup
1 tablespoon rice vinegar or white wine vinegar
2 scallions, thinly sliced
Freshly ground pepper

Calories: 319
Total fat: 7 g
Protein: 12 g
Carbohydrates: 57 g
Fiber: 7 g
Sodium: 715 mg

Creamy Pasta with Asparagus and Peas

Use slender asparagus and you won't need to scrape the stalks. If you still believe that asparagus should be a harbinger of spring (even though it's in the market nearly year-round now), make this dish a tradition by serving it every April or May.

6 SERVINGS

12 ounces farfalle, tricolor rotini, or gemelli

2 tablespoons extra virgin olive oil

2 to 3 garlic cloves, minced

10 to 12 ounces slender asparagus

1 cup frozen green peas

1 medium yellow summer squash, quartered lengthwise and thinly sliced

$1/3$ cup oil-packed sliced sun-dried tomatoes

$1/4$ cup minced fresh parsley

$1/2$ cup Silk creamer

2 tablespoons lemon juice, or more to taste

Salt and freshly ground pepper to taste

Calories: 339
Total fat: 10 g
Protein: 11 g
Carbohydrates: 55 g
Fiber: 6 g
Sodium: 105 mg

1   Cook the pasta in plenty of rapidly simmering water until al dente, then drain.

2   Meanwhile, trim $1/2$ inch from the bottoms of the asparagus spears. Peel the bottom halves only if the stalks are thick; if tender and slim, this won't be necessary. Cut the spears into approximately $1^1/2$-inch lengths.

3   Heat the oil in a wide skillet. Add the garlic and sauté over low heat until golden.

4   Add $1/4$ cup water along with the asparagus, peas, and squash. Cover and cook for 5 minutes, or until the vegetables are just tender-crisp.

5   Add the sun-dried tomatoes, parsley, and creamer. Cook, uncovered, over medium heat until the liquid in the skillet is reduced, about 5 minutes longer.

6   Combine the pasta and vegetables in a large serving bowl. Toss gently but thoroughly. Season with lemon juice, salt, and pepper. Toss again, and serve at once.

Menu suggestions

> A bean-based salad teams well with this delicate dish. Try Black Beans with Tomatoes, Olives, Yellow Peppers, and Croutons (page 185) or Chickpea and Carrot Salad with Parsley and Olives (page 190). Otherwise, any bountiful green salad with the addition of chickpeas, black beans, or pink beans will work well.

> For a hearty pairing with a warm bean dish, see the menu for Dilled Red Beans with Pickled Beets (page 106).

Pasta with Beans and Chard

Swiss chard is a beloved kitchen-garden vegetable in Italian cuisine. Combined with white beans and tomatoes, this stick-to-your-ribs dish will satisfy the heartiest of appetites.

6 SERVINGS

1 good-sized bunch Swiss chard (10 to 12 ounces)

10 to 12 ounces fettuccine or pappardelle

2 tablespoons extra virgin olive oil

1 large onion, quartered and thinly sliced

3 to 4 garlic cloves, minced

1/4 cup dry white wine

One 28-ounce can Italian-style diced or stewed tomatoes, with juice

One 15- to 16-ounce can cannellini or pink beans, drained and rinsed

1/4 cup dark raisins or currants

Salt and freshly ground pepper to taste

Calories: 310
Total fat: 6 g
Protein: 11 g
Carbohydrates: 55 g
Fiber: 7 g
Sodium: 565 mg

1 Remove and discard the stems and thicker midribs from the Swiss chard leaves. Rinse the leaves well, then drain and coarsely chop them.

2 Cook the pasta in plenty of rapidly simmering water until al dente, then drain.

3 Meanwhile, heat the oil in an extra-large saucepan or stir-fry pan. Add the onion and garlic and sauté over medium-low heat until the onion is golden.

4 Add the wine and Swiss chard. Cover and cook just until the chard wilts, stirring once or twice, about 3 minutes.

5 Stir in the tomatoes, beans, and raisins. Cook just until everything is heated through, another 4 to 5 minutes.

6 Combine the fettuccine with the Swiss chard mixture in a large serving bowl. Toss well, season with salt and pepper, and toss again.

Menu suggestions

> I love this dish with cauliflower; two companionable possibilities are Cauliflower with Bread Crumbs (page 206) and Sautéed Cauliflower with Sun-Dried Tomatoes and Basil (page 198). Add a salad of greens, tomatoes, bell peppers, and olives.

> Another good way to complete the meal is with some crusty bread and a dairy-free version of the traditional *insalata caprese* (tomato, mozzarella, and basil salad). Arrange a platter of flavorful tomato slices overlapping thin slices of vegan mozzarella; sprinkle generously with sliced basil leaves and drizzle everything with good olive oil.

Pasta "Carbonara" with Broccoli

Carbonara refers to a dish made with bacon. Here, a bacon substitute in the form of a delicious, smoky tempeh product is used. Look for Lightlife smoky tempeh strips, otherwise known as Fakin' Bacon, in natural food stores and well-stocked supermarkets.

6 SERVINGS

12 ounces pasta, any short chunky shape
2 tablespoons extra virgin olive oil
One 6-ounce package Fakin' Bacon tempeh strips
3 to 4 garlic cloves, minced
4 cups finely chopped broccoli florets
1/2 cup dry white wine
1/4 cup chopped fresh parsley
2 to 4 tablespoons Silk creamer, as needed
Salt and freshly ground pepper to taste

Calories: 332
Total fat: 8 g
Protein: 13 g
Carbohydrates: 51 g
Fiber: 5 g
Sodium: 260 mg

1   Cook the pasta in plenty of rapidly simmering water until al dente, then drain.

2   Meanwhile, heat 1 tablespoon of the oil in a wide skillet. Sauté the "bacon" pieces over medium heat until crisp and browned on both sides, then remove and chop into small squares.

3   In the same skillet, heat the remaining tablespoon of oil. Add the garlic and sauté over low heat until golden.

4   Add the broccoli and wine to the skillet. Cover and steam until the broccoli is bright green and tender-crisp, about 3 minutes. Remove from the heat.

5   In a serving bowl, combine the pasta, tempeh bacon, broccoli-garlic mixture (with any remaining wine), and parsley. Toss well. Add enough creamer to give the dish a bit more moisture. Season with salt and pepper, then serve.

Menu suggestions

> Serve with a salad of dark green lettuce or baby spinach with chickpeas, cherry tomatoes, and red or yellow bell peppers.

> The first two suggestions for mixed baby greens under Recipe Not Required (page 192) go splendidly with this dish. Make Garlic and Lemon Beans (page 110) to boost the protein content of the meal.

Pasta Puttanesca (Pasta with Olive Sauce)

The simplicity of this Neapolitan recipe, named for ladies of the night, belies its luscious flavor. Use pitted olives to ease preparation. I especially like this dish made with whole wheat spaghettini.

1   Cook the pasta in plenty of rapidly simmering water until al dente, then drain.

2   Heat the oil in a large saucepan. Add the garlic and bell pepper and sauté over medium-low heat for 2 to 3 minutes, or until the garlic is golden.

3   Add the fresh tomatoes, sauce, olives, sun-dried tomatoes, and wine. Turn the heat to medium-high and bring to a simmer; then simmer gently, uncovered, for 3 to 5 minutes.

4   Combine the cooked pasta with the olive sauce in a serving bowl. Add the parsley, season with salt and pepper, and toss well. Serve at once.

Menu suggestions

> Serve with Broccoli with Pine Nuts or Almonds (page 204) and a salad of mixed greens or dark green lettuce, chickpeas or red beans, crisp cucumber, and carrots.

> Garlic and Lemon Beans (page 110) is a good way to boost the protein content of the meal. Round it out with a simple slaw or green salad.

> For a hearty meal, start with White Bean and Escarole Soup (page 33). Then choose the Recipe Not Required mixed greens salad that includes pickled beets, crisp cucumber, and turnip (page 192). Top it all off with some crusty whole-grain bread to soak up the delicious flavor.

6 SERVINGS

12 ounces pasta, any long shape of your choice (see headnote)
2 tablespoons extra virgin olive oil
2 to 3 garlic cloves, minced
1 medium red bell pepper, cut into short, narrow strips
1 pound tomatoes, diced
2 cups prepared pasta sauce
3/4 cup pitted brine-cured olives (use a combination of black and green if you like), cut in half
1/4 cup oil-packed sliced sun-dried tomatoes
1/4 cup dry white or red wine
1/4 cup minced fresh parsley
Salt and freshly ground pepper to taste

Calories: 375
Total fat: 10 g
Protein: 10 g
Carbohydrates: 60 g
Fiber: 5 g
Sodium: 790 mg

CHAPTER FIVE

Pizzas, Big Quesadillas, and Wraps

In this brief chapter, you'll find three groupings of sandwich-style meals. We start with pizzas—five really bountiful recipes that focus on produce. Next we move on to what I call "big quesadillas." Unlike the smallish, grilled-cheese-in-a-tortilla specialties you may be more familiar with, those in this chapter are made with the largest size wrappers you can find, and contain nearly an entire meal within their covers. These pizzas and quesadillas are truly the stars of the meal, so my suggestions for completing the menus are minimal. For the most part, nothing pairs better with these pizzas and quesadillas than a salad, though I do make additional suggestions for those times when you want a larger meal, you're serving guests, or teenage male vegans have invaded your home.

Finally, the section on wraps is filled with lists of ingredients that you can mix and match, plus a rundown of wrap ideas that require no formal recipes. When I make wraps, I really don't feel the need to measure exact amounts; it's more fun to just fill, roll, and eat. Sometimes I make one wrap for myself, sometimes I make four for the entire family, and sometimes I make two really enormous wraps and cut them in half to make four. So much depends on the size of the wrappers themselves and on how much of each ingredient you feel like using. Very often, the wrap will actually be the salad portion of the meal. I especially love serving them with soups. In sum, I hope you'll find some uncommon takes on familiar fare in this short but fun-loving chapter.

White Pizza with Sweet Potato and Caramelized Onions

I've suggested in the box on page 141 that most of the pizza recipes in this chapter double easily if you need more servings, with the exception of this one. This is only because it would take an awfully long time to caramelize four large onions. Not that this can't be done, but it wouldn't be a particularly quick meal. However, if time is not an issue and you have a nice large pot for the onions, be my guest and make two of these amazingly delicious pizzas.

MAKES 6 SLICES

1¹/₂ tablespoons olive oil, plus more
  for oiling the pan
2 large onions, quartered and thinly
  sliced
3 to 4 garlic cloves, thinly sliced
1 portobello mushroom, stemmed and
  thinly sliced, optional
1 large sweet potato
One 12.3-ounce package firm silken
  tofu
1 teaspoon salt
One 12- to 14-inch good-quality pizza
  crust
Dried basil

PER SLICE
Calories: 305
Total fat: 6 g
Protein: 12 g
Carbohydrates: 47 g
Fiber: 3 g
Sodium: 650 mg

1   Preheat the oven to 425°F. Lightly oil a small baking pan.

2   Heat the oil in a medium skillet. Add the onions and sauté over medium-low heat until limp. Add the garlic and continue to sauté until the onion is deep golden, stirring frequently, about 15 minutes. If using the portobello, add it after about 10 minutes, continuing to sauté until the slices are softened and the onions golden, stirring occasionally.

3   While the onions are cooking, peel the sweet potato, quarter it lengthwise, and slice it ¹/₄ inch thick. Place the slices in the prepared pan in a single layer. Bake until just tender and lightly roasted, about 15 minutes. Stir every 5 minutes or so.

4   Puree the tofu with the salt in a food processor or with an immersion blender in its container.

5   Place the crust on a baking sheet or pizza stone. Spread the pureed tofu evenly over the crust with a baking spatula. When the onion mixture is done, spread it evenly over the pureed tofu. Bake for 12 to 15 minutes, or until the crust is golden.

6   Scatter the roasted sweet potato pieces over the surface of the pizza. Cut into 6 slices and serve.

Menu suggestions

> To keep the meal really simple, choose one of the green
> salads suggested under Recipe Not Required (page 192).

> If you'd like a pairing that dazzles the eye, try this with
> Broccoli Salad with Yellow Peppers, Pine Nuts, and
> Cranberries (page 182).

> See the menus suggested for Orzo Soup with Roasted
> Vegetables (page 24) or Tomato Chickpea Soup with Tiny
> Pasta and Fresh Herbs (page 32).

White Pizza with Asparagus and Spinach

Here's a lovely, light pizza that's perfect for a springtime meal.

12 asparagus spears

4 to 5 ounces baby spinach

One 12.3-ounce package firm silken tofu

1 teaspoon salt

One 12- to 14-inch good-quality pizza crust

1/3 cup oil-cured sun-dried tomatoes, cut into strips

PER SLICE
Calories: 262
Total fat: 5 g
Protein: 12.5 g
Carbohydrates: 40 g
Fiber: 2 g
Sodium: 685 mg

1 Preheat the oven to 425°F.

2 Trim about an inch from the bottom of the asparagus spears. Scrape the bottom halves if you like, though if they are very slender, this won't be necessary. Cut the spears into 1-inch pieces.

3 Steam the asparagus with a little water in a covered skillet or Dutch oven until bright green and just barely tender-crisp, about 3 minutes.

4 Add the spinach and cover; steam until just wilted, about a minute. Drain the asparagus and spinach well.

5 Puree the tofu with the salt in a food processor or with an immersion blender in its container.

6 Place the crust on a baking sheet or a pizza stone. Spread the tofu puree evenly over the crust with a baking spatula.

7 Scatter the asparagus and spinach evenly over the surface of the pizza, followed by the sun-dried tomatoes. Bake for 12 to 15 minutes, until the crust is golden. Cut into 6 slices and serve.

Menu suggestions

> As with many pizzas, a basic bountiful salad of greens, tomatoes, peppers, cucumbers, and carrots goes well with this.

> If you'd like a heartier salad with this, choose one based on beans. Here are a few possibilities: Black Beans with Tomatoes, Olives, Yellow Peppers, and Croutons (page 185), Black Bean, Mango, and Avocado Salad (page 186), or Chickpea and Carrot Salad with Parsley and Olives (page 190).

> See the menu with Tomato Chickpea Soup with Tiny Pasta and Fresh Herbs (page 32).

Pizza More-than-Margherita

Pizza Margherita is a simple classic, emphasizing fresh tomatoes and basil. This version takes the concept a bit further with a few extra embellishments. It's a wonderful pizza for late summer or for cool summer evenings when you don't mind turning on the oven.

MAKES 6 SLICES

One 12- to 14-inch good-quality pizza crust

3 to 4 medium tomatoes, sliced about 1/4 inch thick

1/3 cup chopped pitted black olives, preferably oil-cured

3/4 cup chopped artichoke hearts (thawed frozen or canned, not marinated)

1/2 cup firm or extra-firm silken tofu, cut into tiny dice

1/4 cup thinly sliced basil leaves, or more to taste

Freshly ground pepper

PER SLICE
Calories: 275
Total fat: 5 g
Protein: 9 g
Carbohydrates: 41 g
Fiber: 2 g
Sodium: 540 mg

1   Preheat the oven to 425°F.

2   Place the crust on a pizza stone or pan. Arrange the tomatoes on the crust in concentric circles, followed by the olives, artichoke hearts, and tofu.

3   Bake for 12 to 15 minutes, until the crust is golden. Scatter the basil over the surface and season with pepper to taste. Cut into 6 wedges to serve.

Menu suggestions

> This is a lighter pizza, so a more substantial salad can be a good choice if you want a heartier meal. Two grain and bean combinations you can choose from are Herb Garden Couscous and Black Bean Salad (page 164) and Quinoa and Red Bean Salad with Crisp Veggies (page 165).

> For a festive meal, pair this with Roasted Summer Vegetable Platter (page 162).

> Since this is a good summer pizza, it's nice served with a cold soup. Cool White Bean and Cucumber Soup (page 38) couldn't be a more perfect choice.

A Note About Serving Sizes for Pizza Recipes

For each of these pizzas, I've designated six slices. Usually that would mean three servings of two slices per person. Some of these pizzas are pretty hearty, and if you're serving them with other foods, it's possible that even one slice may satisfy. I often can't eat more than one, but then I'm a small person. If you're not sure whether six slices will suffice, by all means, double the recipe. They all double fairly easily, with the possible exception of the first one, White Pizza with Sweet Potato and Caramelized Onions (see explanation in the headnote, page 136). Leftover pizza is delightful for lunch the next day and, if it turns out you've made too much, it freezes well. You'll be happy to come across a few slices in your freezer a week or two after you've popped them in there.

Very Green Veggie Pesto Pizza

I'd love to be able to buy a good vegan pesto sauce for those times when I'm too lazy to make one, but so far, I haven't found a brand that doesn't contain cheese. No matter, once you get going, pesto is easy to make, and the one used on this pizza packs a nutritional punch with spinach. This pizza makes a splendid way to get lots of greens in one shot.

MAKES 6 SLICES

1^1/$_2$ tablespoons extra virgin olive oil, plus more for oiling the pan
Spinach-Miso Pesto (page 219)
1^1/$_2$ cups small broccoli florets
1 medium green bell pepper, cut into short, narrow strips
^{3}/$_4$ cup thinly sliced rounds from a small zucchini
3 to 4 garlic cloves, sliced
One 12- to 14-inch good-quality pizza crust
1^1/$_2$ cups grated vegan mozzarella cheese

PER SLICE
Calories: 368
Total fat: 16.5 g
Protein: 11 g
Carbohydrates: 43 g
Fiber: 5 g
Sodium: 595 mg

1   Preheat the oven to 425°F. Lightly oil a roasting pan.

2   Combine the ingredients for the pesto with ^{1}/$_4$ cup water in a food processor. Process until smoothly pureed, stopping the machine and scraping down the sides as needed.

3   Combine the broccoli, bell pepper, zucchini, and garlic in a mixing bowl and drizzle with the olive oil. Stir together. Transfer the vegetables to the prepared pan and put in the oven. Stir after 10 minutes and continue to roast until the vegetables are touched with brown spots here and there.

4   Meanwhile, spread the pesto on the pizza crust and sprinkle evenly with the cheese. Bake for 15 minutes, or until the cheese is nicely melted. Remove from the oven, let stand for a minute, then cut into 6 wedges (it's easier to cut the pizza before piling on the veggies).

5   When the vegetables are done, distribute them evenly over the pizza slices. If the pizza came out of the oven a few minutes before the vegetables, put the whole thing back into the oven for a couple of minutes to get everything piping hot, then serve at once.

Menu suggestions

> While the pizza is baking, you have time to make Chickpea and Carrot Salad with Parsley and Olives (page 190) or, if you prefer, a salad of baby greens with chickpeas, tomatoes, and carrots.

> As an alternative to salad, serve this with a platter of baby carrots (with a creamy vegan dressing as a dip, if you like), cherry or grape tomatoes, and sliced oranges.

> See the menu with Orzo Soup with Roasted Vegetables (page 24).

Sausage, Pepper, Broccoli, and Zucchini Pizza

Piled high with embellishments, this pizza is a good one for hearty appetites.

MAKES 6 SLICES

1½ tablespoons olive oil, plus more
    for the pan
1 link Tofurky sausage, sliced ¼ inch
    thick
1 small red bell pepper, cut into
    narrow strips
1 cup small broccoli florets
1 small zucchini, sliced (or about 1 cup
    halved and sliced zucchini)
2 tablespoons oil-packed sliced sun-
    dried tomatoes, optional
One 12- to 14-inch good-quality pizza
    crust
⅔ cup good-quality pizza or marinara
    sauce of your choice
¾ cup grated vegan Cheddar cheese,
    optional
Dried basil

PER SLICE
Calories: 312
Total fat: 11 g
Protein: 12 g
Carbohydrates: 39 g
Fiber: 3.5 g
Sodium: 445 mg

1   Preheat the oven to 425°F. Lightly oil a roasting pan.

2   Combine the sausage, bell pepper, broccoli, zucchini, optional sun-dried tomatoes, and oil in a mixing bowl. Stir together and transfer to the prepared pan. Place in the hot oven and set a timer for ten minutes.

3   Meanwhile, place the crust on a pizza stone or baking sheet. Distribute the sauce over the crust. Sprinkle with the cheese, if using. Cut the pizza into 6 slices (use a pizza wheel if on a stone; kitchen shears if on a baking sheet). Place the pizza in the oven about 10 minutes after the vegetables.

4   Give the vegetables a stir when the pizza goes in the oven. Bake for an additional 12 to 15 minutes, until the vegetables are nicely roasted and the pizza crust begins to turn golden.

5   Distribute the vegetable mixture evenly over the surface of the pizza, then serve at once.

Menu suggestions

A simple green salad is all that's needed to complete this filling pizza meal. For ideas, see the suggestions for mixed greens salads under Recipe Not Required (page 192), or make a green salad just the way you like it.

Big Quesadillas with Refried Beans, Spinach, and Avocado

Big quesadillas make a filling one-dish meal that is easily completed with a salad on the side. Here is the first of a trio of such fare.

1   Preheat the oven to 425°F.

2   Rinse the greens and steam in a wide skillet or Dutch oven for just a minute or so, until wilted. Transfer to a colander and drain well.

3   Combine the refried beans with a small amount of water in a mixing bowl—just enough to make the beans more spreadable.

4   Lay a tortilla on a baking sheet. Spread one half of it with a quarter of the refried beans, followed by a quarter of the greens and a quarter of the tomato slices. Fold over to cover. Repeat with the remaining tortillas, using an additional baking sheet if needed.

6   Bake for 10 minutes, or until the tortillas begin to turn golden and crisp. Watch carefully!

7   To serve, place each quesadilla or half of a quesadilla on an individual plate. Top with avocado slices. Serve at once, passing around salsa to top individual portions.

Menu suggestions

See the suggestions under Big Quesadillas with Black Beans, Broccoli, and Portobello Mushrooms (page 146). They all work just as well with this quesadilla recipe.

4 LARGE OR 8 SMALLER SERVINGS

4 to 5 ounces arugula or baby spinach
One 15- to 16-ounce can refried beans (any vegan variety)
Four 12-inch flour tortillas or wraps
2 medium firm, ripe tomatoes, halved and sliced
1 medium avocado, sliced
1 cup Pineapple Salsa (page 224) or prepared salsa, or as needed

PER EACH WHOLE QUESADILLA
Calories: 394
Total fat: 13 g
Protein: 13 g
Carbohydrates: 58 g
Fiber: 11 g
Sodium: 735 mg

Big Quesadillas with Black Beans, Broccoli, and Portobello Mushrooms

Bountiful, easy, and filling, these quesadillas entice with the combination of traditional and offbeat ingredients.

4 LARGE OR 8 SMALLER SERVINGS

6 ounces sliced portobello mushrooms

2½ cups small broccoli florets (fresh or frozen; use precut to save time)

Two 15- to 16-ounce cans black beans, drained and rinsed

1 cup salsa (any favorite kind—use something interesting like chipotle)

Four 12-inch flour tortillas or wraps

About 1 cup Instant Roasted Red Pepper Sauce (page 220), or extra salsa

Thinly sliced scallions, optional

PER EACH WHOLE QUESADILLA
Calories: 458
Total fat: 5 g
Protein: 24 g
Carbohydrates: 69 g
Fiber: 17 g
Sodium: 1050 mg

1   Preheat the oven to 425°F.

2   Combine the portobello slices with a small amount of water in a medium skillet; cover and steam until they soften, about 2 minutes. Add the broccoli and continue to steam, covered, until it is bright green and tender-crisp, about 3 minutes longer. Remove from the heat and drain.

3   Combine the beans and salsa in a mixing bowl.

4   Lay a tortilla on a baking sheet. Spread one half of it with a quarter of the black bean mixture, followed by a quarter of the broccoli and mushroom mixture. Fold over to cover. Repeat with the remaining tortillas, using an additional baking sheet if needed.

5   Bake for 10 minutes, or until the tortillas begin to turn golden and crisp. Watch carefully!

6   To serve, place each quesadilla or half of a quesadilla on an individual plate. Top with some of the sauce, then sprinkle with some scallions if desired.

Menu suggestions

> Quick and tasty side dishes for this include Pan-Roasted Corn with Red Peppers and Pumpkin Seeds (page 199) and Zucchini and Summer Squash Sauté (page 209). A simple green salad completes the meal.

> An easy potato side dish is also most welcome alongside this bountiful quesadilla. Since you have the oven going, consider Rosemary Roasted Potatoes with Black Olives (page 195). Start this dish before you start the quesadillas. Other choices include Fingerling Fries (page 194) and Sautéed Paprika Potatoes (page 207). Or simply serve microwaved white or sweet potatoes.

> For a plentiful meal that involves no further recipes, serve only a bountiful green salad and some stone-ground tortilla chips.

Big Quesadillas with Sweet Potato, Yellow Squash, and Corn

When I first blogged about big quesadillas, a number of readers commented about their own fillings. My favorite was this one from Monica Clark-Robinson, an avid and creative cook.

4 LARGE OR 8 SMALLER
SERVINGS

2 medium sweet potatoes
1 medium yellow summer squash
1½ cups frozen corn kernels, thawed
Four 12-inch flour tortillas or wraps
2 cups grated vegan Cheddar or
*   nacho cheese*
1 cup salsa (any variety; salsa verde is
*   delicious with this), or as needed*

PER EACH WHOLE QUESADILLA
Calories: 374
Total fat: 22 g
Protein: 11 g
Carbohydrates: 72 g
Fiber: 12 g
Sodium: 1115 mg

1   Preheat the oven to 425°F.

2   Microwave the sweet potatoes until done but still firm. Start with 2 minutes per potato, then add a minute at a time until they are done. Plunge into a bowl of ice water.

3   Cut the narrow part of the squash into thin rounds. Cut the fatter part of the squash in half, then slice thinly. If there are big, watery seeds, cut them away.

4   Combine the squash with a small amount of water in a medium skillet; cover and steam until partially done, about 2 minutes. Add the corn kernels and continue to steam just until the squash is tender-crisp, then remove from the heat.

5   Peel the sweet potatoes and slice ¼ inch thick.

6   Lay a tortilla on a baking sheet. Arrange a quarter of the sweet potato slices over one half, followed by a quarter of the squash and corn mixture. Sprinkle with ½ cup cheese. Fold over to cover. Repeat with the remaining tortillas, using an additional baking sheet if needed.

7   Bake for 10 minutes, or until the tortillas begin to turn golden and crisp. Watch carefully!

8   To serve, place each quesadilla or half of a quesadilla on an individual plate. Serve at once, passing the salsa to top individual portions.

Menu suggestions

> Black Bean, Mango, and Avocado Salad (page 186) is the perfect companion to these quesadillas. Add some stone-ground tortilla chips, if you like.

> As with the other big quesadillas, you can complete this meal with a bountiful salad and stone-ground tortilla chips to keep things simple.

Recipe Not Required

To Create Your Own Wraps

When it comes to making wraps, I prefer not to use recipes—there's really no need for precise measuring and calculating an exact number of servings. The beauty of these quick sandwich meals is that you can make just one for yourself for a portable lunch or solo dinner or, for a family or group, you can place ingredients on the table and let everyone create their own. Specifying quantities is an inexact science, I find, since the size of the wrappers themselves varies pretty widely, from 10-inch flour tortillas to 15-inch flavored wraps. I have two requirements: the wrappers must be nice and pliable and, of course, all-natural.

Wrapping breads are available in lots of colors and flavors: spinach, sun-dried tomato, garlic and herb; they're also made with various grains, from whole wheat to wheat-free. For express dinners, I love to combine creative wraps with a simple soup, since the salad portion of the meal is often inside the wrap itself. Here are some ingredients that you can mix and match in wraps.

Protein fillings
Refried beans
Hummus
Black, pink, or pinto beans
Baked tofu
Smoked tofu
Sautéed tofu strips
Thinly sliced seitan (sautéed or not)
Sautéed tempeh strips
Sautéed tempeh bacon

Grains
Leftover cooked quinoa
Leftover cooked brown rice
Leftover couscous

Spreads and dressings

Guacamole

Salsa

Vegan Thousand Island dressing

Vegan ranch-style or creamy dill dressing

Vegan mayonnaise

Grainy or yellow mustard

Chutney

Thai peanut satay sauce

Greens and other salad veggies

Baby greens

Baby spinach

Arugula

Green sprouts (such as broccoli sprouts or pea shoots)

Shredded dark green lettuce

Thinly sliced cucumber

Thinly sliced tomatoes

Shredded carrots

Other flavor enhancements

Sun-dried tomatoes (oil-packed or not)

Roasted red peppers

Artichoke hearts (marinated or not)

Easy, Tasty Wraps

Here are some flavorful combinations to use in wraps. Use these ideas to create quick, tasty wraps for brown bag lunches, lunch at home, and nearly instant dinners. Delicious with soup, potato dishes, or sweet potatoes, you can make just one wrap for a solo dinner, or place the ingredients out on the table for a crowd and let everyone make their own.

Hummus and Avocado Wraps

Hummus (store-bought or homemade)

Sliced avocado

Salsa (red or green)

Artichoke hearts (not marinated), optional

Shredded dark green lettuce and/or green sprouts

BBQ Seitan and Avocado Salad Wraps

Strips of seitan, sautéed until lightly browned in a little olive oil
    and a generous amount of natural barbecue sauce

Sliced avocado

Thinly sliced tomatoes

Mixed baby greens

Seitan and Broccoli Wraps

Strips of seitan, sautéed in a little soy sauce and oil

Small broccoli florets, steamed

Thinly shredded dark green lettuce

Green sprouts

Thinly sliced tomatoes

Vegan Thousand Island dressing or vegan mayonnaise

Baked Tofu and Peanut Satay Wraps

Baked tofu, any flavor (try Thai peanut or smoked), cut into
    strips

Jarred roasted red peppers, cut into strips

Thinly sliced cucumber

Thinly shredded dark green lettuce and/or green sprouts

Thai peanut satay sauce

Baked Tofu and Raw Veggie Wraps

Baked tofu, any flavor (try Thai peanut or smoked), cut into
    strips

Red and/or yellow bell peppers, cut into long, narrow strips

Thinly sliced tomatoes

Green sprouts

Vegan creamy dressing (like Nasoya Creamy Dill)

Red and Green Cashew Butter Wraps (use spinach or tomato-flavored
    wraps for these)
Cashew butter
Baby spinach or arugula (raw or lightly wilted)
Roasted red peppers
Sliced sun-dried tomatoes
Sliced ripe tomatoes

Tofu and Black Bean Wraps
Sautéed strips of extra-firm tofu
Black beans
Leftover brown rice or quinoa, optional
Baby greens or shredded dark green lettuce
Salsa

Chutney Lentil Wraps
Leftover brown rice or quinoa
Organic brown or beluga lentils, leftover or canned
Grainy mustard
Vegan mayonnaise
Mango chutney
Baby spinach or arugula

Tempeh Bacon, Greens, and Double Tomato Wraps
Sautéed tempeh bacon
Baby greens, baby lettuce, sprouts, or shredded lettuce,
    or a combination of two
Sliced ripe tomatoes
Sliced sun-dried tomatoes
Vegan mayonnaise

Tempeh Bacon, Portobello Mushroom, and Coleslaw Wraps
Sautéed tempeh bacon
Sautéed sliced portobello mushrooms
Preshredded coleslaw cabbage dressed in vegan mayonnaise or
    vegan creamy dressing of your choice

Spinach, Artichoke, and Chickpea Salad

Tropical Tofu Salad with Chutney Mayonnaise

Asian Edamame and Tofu Chopped Salad

Warm Potato and Black Bean Salad with Red
    Peppers and Artichokes

Gado Gado

Roasted Summer Vegetable Platter

Herb Garden Couscous and Black Bean Salad

Quinoa and Red Bean Salad with Crisp Veggies

Southeast Asian Cold Noodles with Tempeh

Composed Asian Noodle Platter

Hoisin-Flavored Cold Asian Noodles with Crisp
    Vegetables

Salsa, Orzo, and Black Bean Salad

Pasta Salad Niçoise

Pasta Salad with Green Peas, Red Peppers, and
    Cheddar

CHAPTER SIX

Salads with Substance

What transforms a salad from a side dish to a centerpiece? For me, that means combining pasta, legumes, grains, or soy foods—or even two of these—with fresh vegetables (and sometimes fruits), herbs, and a simple dressing. Salad entrees can include anything and everything, as long as the ingredients taste good at room temperature (or chilled) and please both the palate and eye.

If making a meal just for myself, I could easily prepare any of the following recipes with no other accompaniments and be perfectly satisfied. They all contain enough varied elements to make a complete meal. But since I live with three guys, I am aware that not everyone will be satiated by a salad, hearty as these are. So I do suggest menu add-ons to these recipes to create larger meals when desired.

When warm weather hits or you're craving something lighter for dinner, this is a good chapter to explore. As an added bonus, I'll let you in on a little secret—this is the chapter I've turned to most often recently to find a dish to share at potlucks and other gatherings. Many of these salads look highly appetizing and keep well for hours at room temperature— perfect qualities for food intended for sharing.

Spinach, Artichoke, and Chickpea Salad

A feast of color and texture, this salad is, in a word, dazzling. As the centerpiece of a meal, it's a pleasure to make and serve, ready in minutes.

4 TO 6 SERVINGS

4 to 6 ounces baby spinach

One 15-ounce can artichokes, drained and cut in half

1 cup thinly sliced red cabbage

1/3 cup oil-cured black olives

1 cup drained and rinsed canned chickpeas

1 cup cherry tomatoes, cut in half

1/2 cup baby carrots, cut in half lengthwise

1/2 cup drained and sliced jarred roasted red or yellow peppers

2 to 3 tablespoons sunflower seeds

2 tablespoons extra virgin olive oil or flaxseed oil

Lemon juice to taste

Calories: 285
Total fat: 14 g
Protein: 9 g
Carbohydrates: 32 g
Fiber: 12.5 g
Sodium: 415 mg

Combine all the ingredients in a serving bowl and toss well. Serve at once.

Variation   Substitute arugula and/or mixed baby greens for all or part of the spinach.

Menu suggestions

> For a hearty salad and sandwich meal, serve with Seitan Gyros (page 72) or Tempeh Bacon, Portobello Mushroom, and Coleslaw Wraps (page 153).

> This salad pairs well with a light grain dish to make a complete meal. A good companion is Lemony Couscous with Broccoli (page 94) or Quinoa with Corn and Scallions (page 91).

> For a stove-free summer meal, serve this with Fresh Tomato-Coconut Soup (page 39) and fresh bread.

Tropical Tofu Salad with Chutney Mayonnaise

I love this salad with mango, but since it's not always available, pineapple is a good alternative. If you have more time, use fresh pineapple in season. Cutting it up is really not that time consuming, and the fresh fruit tastes amazing.

1   Steam the broccoli in a large saucepan until bright green and just tender-crisp, about 3 minutes. Transfer to a colander and rinse with cool water until the broccoli stops steaming.

2   In a mixing bowl, combine the broccoli with the tofu, mango, celery, and optional walnuts. Stir together.

3   Combine the mayonnaise and chutney in a small bowl and stir until smoothly blended. Pour into the salad and toss gently.

4   To serve, divide the greens among individual plates, mound a small amount of the salad on each, and top with some sprouts.

Menu suggestions

> This is delicious served with Coconut-Curry Bean Thread Noodles (page 115) for a meal that's not just about salad.

> Pair with one of the simple Asian-style noodle side dishes under Easy Ways to Dress Up Pasta and Noodle Side Dishes (page 121).

4 TO 6 SERVINGS

1 large broccoli crown, cut into small florets

Two 8-ounce packages baked tofu, diced or cut into strips

2 medium mangos, peeled and diced, or one 20-ounce can diced pineapple, well drained

2 large celery stalks, sliced diagonally

1/3 cup chopped walnuts, optional

1/3 cup vegan mayonnaise

1/3 cup mango chutney or other fruit chutney

Mixed baby greens, as needed

Green sprouts (sweet pea shoots, broccoli or other sprouts), as needed

Calories: 430
Total fat: 21 g
Protein: 26 g
Carbohydrates: 40 g
Fiber: 5 g
Sodium: 800 mg

Asian Edamame and Tofu Chopped Salad

This was inspired by one of my favorite dishes at Veggie Heaven in Teaneck, New Jersey, an all-vegan Chinese-style eatery. It's quite unlike their signature mock meat dishes, and really, quite unlike anything I have ever eaten in an Asian restaurant.

4 TO 6 SERVINGS

1 cup frozen edamame, thawed

1/4 cup pine nuts

1 small zucchini, cut into 1/4-inch dice (about 1 cup)

1 small red or orange bell pepper, cut into 1/4-inch dice

2 large celery stalks, cut into 1/4-inch dice

4 to 5 ounces baked tofu, cut into 1/4-inch dice

1/4 cup thinly sliced scallions, green parts only

2 tablespoons olive oil

2 teaspoons dark sesame oil

2 tablespoons rice vinegar

Salt and freshly ground pepper to taste

Calories: 330
Total fat: 25 g
Protein: 17 g
Carbohydrates: 14 g
Fiber: 4 g
Sodium: 160 mg

1 Cook the edamame according to package directions, then drain and rinse in a colander until cool.

2 Toast the pine nuts in a small, dry skillet over medium heat until golden.

3 Combine the edamame and pine nuts with the remaining ingredients in a serving bowl and toss together. Serve at once.

Menu suggestions

> See the menu with Tomato-Coconut Soup (page 39). Complete the meal with store-bought vegan spring rolls or corn on the cob.

> This teams nicely with Gingery Rice with Sweet Potatoes and Peas (page 88). Add a simple salad of greens and tomatoes or any of the Recipe Not Required mixed greens salads (page 192).

> To complete the meal with no additional recipes, make one of the Asian-style noodle side dishes under Easy Ways to Dress Up Pasta and Noodle Side Dishes (page 121). Add a platter of cherry tomatoes, baby corn, and sliced cucumbers.

Warm Potato and Black Bean Salad with Red Peppers and Artichokes

Potatoes and black beans synergize nicely in this offbeat salad. The liquid from the artichoke hearts provides plenty of flavor.

1 Microwave the potatoes until done but still firm, about 2 minutes per potato. Plunge into a bowl of cool water until just cool enough to handle, but still warm.

2 Combine the beans, artichoke hearts, bell pepper, parsley, and scallions in a serving bowl.

3 Peel and dice the potatoes and add them to the bean mixture, then toss with the lemon juice. Season with salt and pepper.

4 Serve at once, while the potatoes are still warm. Place each serving on a small bed of greens and sprinkle with some seeds, if desired.

Variation Replace half of the potatoes with sweet potato. Microwave the sweet potato separately until done but still nice and firm.

Menu suggestions

> For a tasty summer meal, serve this with Mediterranean Tofu (page 42) or Tempeh Fries (page 78) and a platter of sliced ripe tomatoes and basil strips drizzled with olive oil.

> Make a batch of BBQ-Flavored Skillet Tofu (page 62) and serve with a platter of tomatoes prepared as suggested above.

4 TO 6 SERVINGS

4 to 5 medium red-skinned or Yukon gold potatoes

One 15- to 16-ounce can black beans, drained and rinsed

One 6- to 8-ounce jar marinated artichoke hearts, chopped, with liquid

One medium red bell pepper, cut into short, narrow strips

1/4 cup minced fresh parsley

2 scallions, green parts only, thinly sliced

2 tablespoons lemon juice, or more to taste

Salt and freshly ground pepper to taste

Mixed baby greens, optional

Pumpkin or sunflower seeds, optional

Calories: 208
Total fat: 4 g
Protein: 9 g
Carbohydrates: 36 g
Fiber: 4 g
Sodium: 460 mg

Gado Gado

I'll always have a pleasant association with this classic Indonesian salad platter, as it was the first meal I had on my first trip to Paris. The tiny, cozy Indonesian restaurant was right next door to our hotel, and coming straight from an all-night flight, my friend Wendy and I were too tired to venture further before a meal and a nap. Served with plenty of rice, the salad (which always combines raw and lightly cooked vegetables) made for a filling and memorable meal. Here's my Americanized, but still appealing interpretation.

4 SERVINGS

2 to 3 ounces mixed baby greens

1 cup green sprouts, such as sweet pea shoots or broccoli sprouts

4 ounces slender green beans (see Note)

1/2 medium head cauliflower, cut into bite-size pieces

1 cup baby carrots (thick ones cut in half lengthwise)

3 medium tomatoes, diced, or 1 cup cherry tomatoes

Two 8-ounce packages Thai-style or smoked baked tofu, thinly sliced

3/4 cup Coconut-Peanut Sauce or Salad Dressing (page 215), or as needed

Calories: 378
Total fat: 15 g
Protein: 26 g
Carbohydrates: 30 g
Fiber: 9 g
Sodium: 630 mg

1 Spread the greens on a large serving platter and sprinkle the sprouts over them.

2 Place the green beans, cauliflower, and carrots side by side, without mixing, in a wide skillet with about 1/4 inch of water. Cover and steam for 3 to 4 minutes, or until all are tender-crisp. Remove each type of vegetable separately with a slotted spoon, transfer to a colander, and refresh under cool water. Transfer each vegetable to a small plate.

3 Arrange the green beans, cauliflower, and carrots in separate mounds on the greens, leaving room to add the tomatoes and tofu. Arrange those on the greens as well, between the cooked vegetables.

4 To serve, let everyone scoop the vegetables, tofu, and greens onto individual plates, then pass the dressing for everyone to use as desired.

Note   As I've suggested in other places in this book, if fresh slender green beans are unavailable, substitute frozen whole organic baby green beans.

Menu suggestions

The beauty of this salad platter is that it contains nearly all the elements of a well-rounded meal: raw and cooked veggies, tofu, and a high-protein sauce. All it needs are some high-quality carbs like cooked brown rice. Or, if you're in more of a hurry, choose one of the Asian-style noodle side dishes under Easy Ways to Dress Up Pasta and Noodle Side Dishes (page 121).

Roasted Summer Vegetable Platter

This is one of my favorite things to make in the late summer—a gorgeous platter that's really less work than it may seem at first glance. It's an extravaganza of flavor, and though it's perfect for late summer or early fall, with these particular veggies there's no reason you can't make it year-round.

6 OR MORE SERVINGS

Marinade
2 tablespoons extra virgin olive oil
2 tablespoons balsamic vinegar
1/4 cup dry white wine
1 teaspoon salt-free seasoning (such as Spike or Mrs. Dash)
1/2 teaspoon dried oregano

2 long Japanese eggplants (about 1 pound), sliced (see Note)
1/2 medium zucchini, sliced
1/2 medium yellow summer squash, sliced
1 medium green bell pepper, cut into rings
1 medium red bell pepper, cut to match green pepper
1/3 cup oil-packed sun-dried tomatoes, cut into strips, plus 1 tablespoon of their oil
Salt and freshly ground pepper to taste
2 to 3 ounces mixed baby greens

Calories: 132
Total fat: 9 g
Protein: 2 g
Carbohydrates: 13 g
Fiber: 4 g
Sodium: 40 mg

1   Preheat the oven to 450°F. Line a roasting pan with foil.

2   Combine the ingredients for the marinade in a small bowl and stir together.

3   Combine the eggplants, squashes, and peppers in a large mixing bowl. Pour the marinade over them and toss.

4   Transfer the vegetables with the marinade to the lined pan. Roast for 20 to 25 minutes, stirring after the first 10 minutes and then every 5 minutes thereafter, until the vegetables are tender and lightly browned.

5   Remove from the oven and transfer back into the mixing bowl. Stir in the sun-dried tomatoes and their oil. Season with salt and pepper.

6   Line a large platter with the baby greens. Arrange the roasted vegetables over them. Serve at once, or let cool to room temperature before serving.

Note If you can't find Japanese eggplants, substitute any small eggplant (try white or the magenta and white streaked varieties), halved lengthwise and sliced.

Menu suggestions

> For a summer meal, make a quick cool soup that requires little hands-on time while the vegetables are roasting. Two good ones to go with this are Curried Cashew and Green Pea Soup (page 28) and Cool White Bean and Cucumber Soup (page 38). Serve the meal with ripe summer tomatoes and fresh bread.

> Roast a batch of Teriyaki Tofu Steaks (page 62) or Cornmeal-Crusted Tofu (page 62) in the oven while the vegetables are roasting. Add some cherry tomatoes and baby carrots to each plate and, if you like, some corn on the cob as well.

Herb Garden Couscous and Black Bean Salad

This recipe is one I've used for a long time, though oddly, it has never made it into any of my books until now. It's an attractive, fast main dish salad that can be made all year round (now that fresh herbs of all kinds are always available in any supermarket), though I still prefer serving it during warmer months. Leftovers of this salad are delicious in a wrap the next day for lunch or dinner.

6 SERVINGS

1 cup couscous
One 15- to 16-ounce can black beans, drained and rinsed
1 large celery stalk, diced
1 medium red or orange bell pepper, diced
1 cup grape tomatoes
1/4 cup chopped green olives
1/2 cup chopped fresh parsley
2 tablespoons chopped fresh dill
Several fresh mint leaves, sliced
2 scallions, green parts only, finely chopped
2 tablespoons lemon juice
2 tablespoons extra virgin olive oil
Salt and freshly ground pepper to taste
Butter, Boston, or Bibb lettuce leaves

Calories: 237
Total fat: 7 g
Protein: 8.5 g
Carbohydrates: 36 g
Fiber: 7 g
Sodium: 420 mg

1   In a large heatproof container, combine the couscous with 2 cups boiling water. Cover and let stand for 10 minutes, then uncover and fluff with a fork.

2   Let cool, uncovered, for 5 minutes, then stir in the remaining ingredients except for the lettuce.

3   Serve warm or at room temperature, arranging some of the salad over a few lettuce leaves for each serving.

Menu suggestion

>   When I want to keep a salad theme going, I serve this with Great Grated Veggies with Tahini Dressing (page 175) or Mixed Greens with Sprouts, Apple, and Daikon (page 179).

>   For a heartier meal, serve with with veggie burgers and one of the suggestions for mixed greens salads under Recipe Not Required (page 192).

Quinoa and Red Bean Salad with Crisp Veggies

Like the previous recipe, the combination of grains and beans in this salad makes it an ideal centerpiece for a meal.

1   Combine the quinoa with 1^1/2 cups water in a small saucepan and bring to a rapid simmer, then lower the heat. Cover and simmer gently for 15 minutes, or until the water is absorbed. Transfer the quinoa to a wide bowl or casserole dish so that it can cool quickly.

2   Meanwhile, place the tomatoes, turnip, pepper, carrots, and olives in a serving bowl.

3   When the quinoa is just warm, add it to the vegetables along with the beans, dill to taste, and dressing; toss together. Season with salt and pepper, then serve.

Menu suggestions

> A green vegetable side dish enhances this hearty salad nicely. Try it with Sautéed Asparagus with Almonds (page 203), any of the broccoli side dishes on page 204, or Zucchini and Polenta Marinara (page 200). Add sautéed soy sausage links or BBQ-Flavored Skillet Tofu (page 62) if you'd like a larger meal.

> For a filling meal, pair this with Smashed Sweet Potatoes with Cashew Butter Sauce (page 209) and steamed broccoli, Brussels sprouts, or green beans.

6 SERVINGS

^{3}/4 cup quinoa, rinsed in a fine sieve

1 cup halved yellow or red cherry tomatoes

^{1}/2 cup peeled, diced turnip or daikon radish

^{1}/2 medium orange or yellow bell pepper, diced

8 baby carrots, quartered lengthwise

^{1}/3 cup chopped black olives

One 15- to 16-ounce can small red beans, drained and rinsed

2 to 3 tablespoons minced fresh dill

^{1}/2 cup Salsa and Olive Oil Salad Dressing (page 223), or as needed

Salt and freshly ground pepper to taste

Calories: 245
Total fat: 8 g
Protein: 8 g
Carbohydrates: 36 g
Fiber: 6.5 g
Sodium: 65 mg

Southeast Asian Cold Noodles with Tempeh

This spicy, nutty salad is an amalgam of Indonesian and Thai-influenced ingredients and seasonings.

6 TO 8 SERVINGS

8 ounces udon or other Asian noodles of your choice

One 12-ounce package tempeh

1 tablespoon light olive oil

1 tablespoon reduced-sodium soy sauce

Chili powder

2 cups small broccoli florets

6 large baby carrots, quartered lengthwise

3 scallions, green parts only, sliced

1/4 cup chopped fresh cilantro or parsley

1/4 cup crushed peanuts, optional

1/2 cup Thai peanut satay sauce

2 tablespoons lime juice, or to taste

Calories: 375
Total fat: 14 g
Protein: 20 g
Carbohydrates: 42 g
Fiber: 4 g
Sodium: 240 mg

1   Cook the noodles in plenty of rapidly simmering water until al dente. Drain and rinse under cool water, then drain well again.

2   Cut the tempeh into 1/2-inch dice. Slowly heat the oil and soy sauce together in a wide skillet. Add the tempeh and sauté over medium heat, stirring frequently, until nicely browned and crisp. Sprinkle lightly with chili powder to taste and remove from the heat.

3   Meanwhile, steam the broccoli and carrots in a large saucepan with about 1/2 inch of water until just tender-crisp, about 3 minutes. Drain and rinse under cool water, then drain well again.

4   Combine the noodles, broccoli, and carrots in a serving bowl. Add the tempeh, scallions, cilantro, and optional peanuts. Pour in the satay sauce and lime juice, toss well, and serve.

Menu suggestions

> I like this served side by side with a simple, refreshing salad such as Bok Choy, Red Cabbage, and Carrot Salad (page 176) or Mixed Greens with Sprouts, Apple, and Daikon (page 179). Store-bought vegan spring rolls or dumplings are a fun way to round out the meal.

> An interesting companion dish is Bell Pepper and Bok Choy Stir-Fry (page 204). Add a platter of grape or cherry tomatoes and sliced cucumbers.

Composed Asian Noodle Platter

This colorful mélange of flavors and textures is easy enough for a weeknight meal, yet gorgeous enough to impress guests.

1   In a heatproof container, cover the noodles with very hot water. Cover the dish and let the noodles soak for 15 to 20 minutes or until al dente, then drain. Rinse under cool water, then drain well again. Cut the noodles in several directions to shorten (kitchen shears work well for this).

2   Meanwhile, combine the spinach, bok choy, and cabbage in a mixing bowl. Spread on a large serving platter.

3   Combine the cooked noodles with $1/2$ cup of the peanut sauce, the cilantro, and half of the scallions. Toss together.

4   To arrange the salad, mound the noodle mixture in the center of the vegetables, leaving about 3 inches of the vegetables showing all around. Arrange a neat pile of half of the tofu on one side of the vegetables, and the other half opposite. Do the same with the pepper. Scatter the remaining scallions over the top, followed by the optional peanuts.

5   Pass the salad around with salad tongs for grabbing the salad components. Pass additional dressing for everyone to use as desired.

Menu suggestions

A light soup is a good introduction to this centerpiece salad. Fresh Tomato-Coconut Soup (page 39) is a nice summer selection, and for cooler weather, try Miso Soup with Sweet Potatoes and Watercress (page 36).

4 SERVINGS

4 ounces Asian rice vermicelli or bean thread noodles

3 to 4 ounces baby spinach, long stems removed if desired

3 stalks bok choy, with leaves, thinly sliced

1 cup thinly shredded red cabbage

$3/4$ cup Coconut-Peanut Sauce or Salad Dressing (page 215), or as needed

$1/4$ cup minced fresh cilantro

3 to 4 scallions, green parts only, thinly sliced

One 8-ounce package White Wave Thai baked tofu, cut into thin strips

1 red bell pepper, cut into short, narrow strips

$1/4$ cup peanut halves, optional

Calories: 228
Total fat: 11 g
Protein: 13 g
Carbohydrates: 38 g
Fiber: 4 g
Sodium: 445 mg

Hoisin-Flavored Cold Asian Noodles with Crisp Vegetables

Crunchy and colorful, this is an appealing presentation for cold Asian noodles.

4 TO 6 SERVINGS

Dressing

2 tablespoons reduced-sodium soy sauce, or to taste

3 tablespoons rice vinegar

2 tablespoons hoisin sauce

2 tablespoons light olive oil

1 teaspoon dark sesame oil

8 ounces Chinese wheat noodles, udon noodles, or soba

3 stalks bok choy, sliced on the diagonal

One 15-ounce can baby corn, drained, a little liquid reserved

8 baby carrots, quartered lengthwise

4 to 6 ounces snow peas or snap peas

2 to 3 scallions, green parts only, thinly sliced

1/4 cup minced fresh cilantro, or more to taste, optional

1/3 cup chopped toasted cashews

Calories: 389
Total fat: 15 g
Protein: 12 g
Carbohydrates: 53 g
Fiber: 7 g
Sodium: 710 mg

1 Combine the dressing ingredients in a small bowl and stir together. Set aside.

2 Cook the noodles in plenty of rapidly simmering water until al dente. Drain and rinse under cool water, then drain well again.

3 Meanwhile, combine the remaining ingredients in a large serving bowl. Add the cooked noodles and dressing, and toss well. If the mixture needs a bit more moisture, drizzle in a small amount of the reserved liquid from the baby corn. Cover and refrigerate until needed, or serve at once.

Menu suggestions

> Two good companion dishes for extra protein are Cornmeal-Crusted Seitan (page 63) and Tempeh Fries with Horseradish or Wasabi-Dill Mayonnaise (page 78). Add cherry tomatoes or sliced tomatoes to the plate.

> For a light meal, serve this salad with Sautéed Tofu (page 62) and steamed broccoli.

Salsa, Orzo, and Black Bean Salad

Bursting with Southwestern flavors, this salad is as delicious as it is easy.

1   Cook the orzo in plenty of rapidly simmering water until al dente. Drain and rinse until cool, then drain well again.

2   Meanwhile, combine the remaining ingredients in a serving bowl. Add the cooked orzo and toss together. Check the seasoning and serve.

Menu suggestions

>   This is a pleasant accompaniment to Tofu Rancheros (page 58). Embellish the plates with sliced avocados and oranges.

>   Serve with Quinoa with Corn and Scallions (page 91) and a salad of mixed greens, tomatoes, avocado, and olives.

6 SERVINGS

1 cup orzo (rice-shaped pasta)

One 15- to 16-ounce can black beans, drained and rinsed

1 cup frozen or fresh corn kernels, cooked

$1/2$ medium green or red bell pepper, finely diced

1 cup prepared salsa, any interesting flavor (try chipotle or cilantro-garlic)

$1/4$ to $1/2$ chopped fresh cilantro

2 to 3 scallions, green parts only, thinly sliced

2 tablespoons extra virgin olive oil

1 teaspoon ground cumin

2 tablespoons lemon or lime juice, or more to taste

Salt and freshly ground pepper to taste

Calories: 272
Total fat: 6 g
Protein: 10.5 g
Carbohydrates: 45 g
Fiber: 8 g
Sodium: 280 mg

Pasta Salad Niçoise

The ingredients of salade Niçoise—green beans, white beans, ripe tomatoes, and cured olives—join forces with pasta to make a delectable cold dish. Baked tofu stands in for tuna, another standard Niçoise ingredient.

Dressing
2 tablespoons extra virgin olive oil
1/4 cup red wine vinegar
2 teaspoons Dijon-style mustard
1/2 teaspoon dried basil

8 to 10 ounces pasta, any short shape
2 cups fresh green beans, cut into 1-inch lengths, or frozen cut green beans, thawed
1 cup drained and rinsed canned cannellini beans
2 medium tomatoes, diced
One 8-ounce package baked tofu, any flavor (try smoked or lemon-pepper), finely diced
1/3 cup Niçoise or other brine-cured olives
1/4 cup minced fresh parsley
Salt and freshly ground pepper to taste

Calories: 340
Total fat: 12 g
Protein: 15 g
Carbohydrates: 44 g
Fiber: 4.5 g
Sodium: 545 mg

1   Combine the dressing ingredients in a small bowl and stir until well blended. Set aside.

2   Cook the pasta in plenty of rapidly simmering water until al dente. Drain and rinse until cool, then drain well again.

3   Steam the green beans in a medium saucepan with a small amount of water until tender-crisp. Drain and rinse under cool water.

4   Combine the pasta, green beans, and dressing in a large serving bowl along with the remaining salad ingredients, and toss together. Serve at room temperature.

Menu suggestions

This salad contains so many elements of a meal that little else is needed to make it complete. In summer, corn on the cob is an easy companion. At other times of the year, quick vegetable dishes you can choose from include Sautéed Cauliflower with Sun-Dried Tomatoes and Basil (page 198), Mediterranean Spinach with Pine Nuts and Raisins (page 202), and Zucchini and Summer Squash Sauté (page 209).

Pasta Salad with Green Peas, Red Peppers, and Cheddar

Years ago, as vegetarians, my husband and I traveled through the American heartland, and I remember sampling a traditional salad whose main ingredients are green peas and Cheddar cheese. I expanded this basic formula (as well as the foggy memory) into a recipe that includes pasta, making it more substantial.

1   Cook the pasta in plenty of rapidly simmering water until al dente. When the pasta is almost done, add the peas and cook briefly. Drain and rinse until cool, then drain well again.

2   Toss the pasta and peas with the remaining ingredients. Serve at once.

Menu suggestions

> I love this with Red and Green Cashew Butter Wraps (page 153).

> This is also a great companion to veggie burgers with all the fixings—lettuce, tomato, vegan mayonnaise, and mustard—for a carefree meal.

6 SERVINGS

8 to 10 ounces pasta, any short shape (try gemelli or farfalle)

$1^1/2$ cups frozen green peas

1 large red bell pepper, cut into narrow strips

$1/3$ cup pitted black olives, preferably oil-cured

1 large celery stalk, diced

5 or 6 radishes, thinly sliced, or $1/3$ cup thinly sliced daikon radish, cut into half circles

1 cup diced vegan Cheddar cheese

$1/4$ cup minced fresh parsley or dill, or a combination

$1/2$ cup Salsa and Olive Oil Salad Dressing (page 223), or $1/3$ cup vinaigrette, homemade (page 221), or store-bought

Salt and freshly ground pepper to taste

Calories: 350
Total fat: 17 g
Protein: 8 g
Carbohydrates: 40 g
Fiber: 5.5 g
Sodium: 350 mg

Grated Daikon and Carrot Salad

Great Grated Veggies with Tahini Dressing

Bok Choy, Red Cabbage, and Carrot Salad

Fruitful Red Slaw

Creole Coleslaw

Mixed Greens with Sprouts, Apple, and Daikon

Spinach and Red Cabbage Salad with Oranges and
Almonds

Tri-Color Sweet and Tangy Peppers

Broccoli Salad with Yellow Peppers, Pine Nuts, and
Cranberries

Quinoa Tabouleh with Pine Nuts

Thai Tossed Salad

Black Beans with Tomatoes, Olives, Yellow Peppers,
and Croutons

Black Bean, Mango, and Avocado Salad

Salade Janine

Sweet and White Potato Salad with Mixed Greens

Cauliflower and Carrot Salad

Chickpea and Carrot Salad with Parsley and Olives

Middle Eastern Chopped Salad

Warm Mediterranean Potato Salad

Fingerling Fries

Rosemary Roasted Potatoes with Black Olives

Spanish Bell Pepper Sauté

Spicy Sesame Broccoli

Sautéed Cauliflower with Sun-Dried Tomatoes and
Basil

Pan-Roasted Corn with Red Peppers and Pumpkin
Seeds

Zucchini and Polenta Marinara

Garlicky Greens

Mediterranean Spinach with Pine Nuts and Raisins

CHAPTER SEVEN

Salads and Veggies on the Side

The salads in this chapter aim to be just as appealing as the centerpiece salads in Chapter Six, though these are designed as companion dishes, rather than as the focus of a meal. Hearty, high-protein salads like Black Beans with Tomatoes, Olives, Yellow Peppers, and Croutons (page 185) or Quinoa Tabouleh with Pine Nuts (page 183) can almost serve as meals if served in large enough quantities, but I also enjoy how they play off other dishes. Still, there are times when I'll choose one of these salads first, then decide what main dish or companion dish (such as a soup or wrap) will work well with it. During warm months, it's also fun to compose meals of several smaller cool dishes, rather than having one centerpiece. No matter how you use them, these salads add color, variety, and a myriad of raw vegetables (and sometimes fruit) to your quick meals.

The second half of this chapter offers a variety of easy side dishes for everyday vegetables, starting on page 194 with a few formal (but simple) recipes, and ending with a rundown of my own favorite ways to embellish vegetable sides without much fuss. Broccoli is fine on its own, but it's even better with a sprinkling of pine nuts; cauliflower is that much more enjoyable with bread crumbs, and so on. Most vegans and vegetarians don't need a lot of prodding to eat their veggies, but with these ideas, you're likely to indulge in even more of a good thing.

173

Grated Daikon and Carrot Salad

The word *daikon* actually comes from two Japanese words, *dai* (large) and *kon* (root). And that's just what it is. Daikon radish, a large white root vegetable, is often served grated in small quantities with Asian meals, since it's considered a good digestive aid. I often combine it with one or two other vegetables—if one, that would be carrots, as presented here, and if two, I'll also grate any broccoli stem I've saved in the fridge. It's a refreshing little salad that goes with just about any kind of meal.

4 TO 6 SERVINGS

1 large daikon radish
2 medium carrots
2 tablespoons flaxseed oil
2 tablespoons lemon juice
1 teaspoon agave nectar or natural granulated sugar
¼ teaspoon dried dill
Salt and freshly ground pepper to taste

Calories: 97
Total fat: 7 g
Protein: 1 g
Carbohydrates: 9 g
Fiber: 2 g
Sodium: 30 mg

1   Cut the daikon and carrots into chunks and grate in a food processor.

2   Transfer to a serving bowl, add the remaining ingredients, and toss together. Serve at once.

Variation   Grate the daikon radish and carrot separately and put into two small serving bowls. Divide the remaining ingredients evenly between them. Serve side by side.

Great Grated Veggies with Tahini Dressing

Here's another good way to utilize root vegetables raw; the dressing adds a rich, delicious flavor.

1   Combine the dressing ingredients in a small bowl and stir together.

2   Place the grated vegetables and dressing in a serving bowl. Toss until completely combined. Season with salt and pepper and toss again. Serve at once.

6 SERVINGS

Dressing

1 1/2 tablespoons tahini (sesame paste)

2 to 3 tablespoons lemon juice, to taste

1 tablespoon agave nectar

2 tablespoons vegan mayonnaise

1 tablespoon minced fresh dill or 1/4 teaspoon dried

4 cups grated raw vegetables (use a combination of trimmed and peeled broccoli stems, carrots, turnip, jicama, golden beets, and daikon radish—choose 2 or 3)

Salt and freshly ground pepper to taste

Calories: 70
Total fat: 3.5 g
Protein: 2 g
Carbohydrates: 10 g
Fiber: 3 g
Sodium: 60 mg

Bok Choy, Red Cabbage, and Carrot Salad

This crisp salad is a delightful accompaniment to many Asian-style grain, noodle, tofu, or seitan dishes. I recommend it quite often throughout the book.

4 TO 6 SERVINGS

4 medium stalks bok choy (with leaves), thinly sliced on the diagonal

2 cups thinly shredded red cabbage

2 medium carrots, thinly sliced on the diagonal

2 scallions, green parts only, thinly sliced

1/4 cup cilantro leaves, optional

1/4 cup toasted sliced or slivered almonds

1/4 cup Sesame-Ginger Salad Dressing (page 222) or store-bought equivalent, or as needed to moisten

Calories: 125
Total fat: 10 g
Protein: 2.5 g
Carbohydrates: 9 g
Fiber: 2 g
Sodium: 60 mg

Combine all the ingredients in a serving bowl and toss together. Let stand for 5 to 10 minutes before serving.

Fruitful Red Slaw

When you need to add color and crunch to a dinner plate, this fruit-filled slaw is a pleasing option. I like using Granny Smith apples in this recipe, but use any crisp apple you have on hand. Make this salad before starting your meal's centerpiece; it benefits from having time to let the flavors blend and the cabbage soften.

Combine all of the ingredients in a serving bowl and stir together. Let stand for 15 minutes or so before serving.

2 cups coarsely shredded red cabbage

8 baby carrots, quartered lengthwise

2 medium crisp apples, thinly sliced

$1/2$ cup diced mango or pineapple, or halved red or green seedless grapes

$1/4$ cup toasted pine nuts or $1/3$ cup finely chopped walnuts or almonds

2 tablespoons flaxseed or olive oil

2 tablespoons lemon or lime juice, or to taste

1 tablespoon sesame seeds

Calories: 127
Total fat: 8 g
Protein: 2 g
Carbohydrates: 14 g
Fiber: 3 g
Sodium: 10 mg

SALADS AND VEGGIES ON THE SIDE

VEGAN EXPRESS

Creole Coleslaw

Crushed pineapple is the standout ingredient in this pleasant slaw. It provides a good balance to spicy or bold dishes. I like it with Southwestern fare like Tortilla Casserole (page 104), but my favorite dish to serve it with is Pasta Jambalaya (page 123).

4 TO 6 SERVINGS

1/4 cup vegan mayonnaise

2 tablespoons sweet pickle relish

1 teaspoon yellow mustard

2 cups shredded green cabbage

2 cups shredded red cabbage

8 baby carrots, quartered lengthwise

1/2 cup crushed or finely diced pineapple (fresh or canned)

Salt and freshly ground pepper to taste

Calories: 87
Total fat: 4 g
Protein: 2 g
Carbohydrates: 13 g
Fiber: 3 g
Sodium: 215 mg

1   Combine the mayonnaise, relish, and mustard in a small bowl. Stir until blended.

2   Combine the cabbages, carrots, and pineapple in a serving bowl and toss together. Pour the dressing over the vegetables and mix well. Season with salt and pepper and serve.

Mixed Greens with Sprouts, Apple, and Daikon

Not only is this salad refreshing, it also contains many ingredients valued for their cleansing properties. Its fresh flavor is especially enticing to me in the spring, but it's welcome all year round; in fact, I recommend this salad frequently throughout the book. I often make it when I want a refreshing contrast to a hearty, spicy, or bold dish.

Combine all of the ingredients in a serving bowl, toss, and serve.

Variation   Add two small raw golden beets, peeled and thinly sliced into half circles.

4 TO 6 SERVINGS

4 to 6 ounces tender greens (baby greens, arugula, baby spinach, watercress, or a mixture)

1 cup green sprouts (such as sweet pea shoots or broccoli sprouts)

1 Granny Smith apple, diced

1/2 medium daikon radish, sliced

2 large stalks celery or bok choy, sliced

1/2 medium cucumber, unpeeled, cut in half lengthwise and sliced

1 1/2 tablespoons flaxseed or olive oil

2 tablespoons lemon juice, or to taste

1/4 cup toasted pumpkin seeds, optional

Calories: 140
Total fat: 6 g
Protein: 4 g
Carbohydrates: 20 g
Fiber: 4 g
Sodium: 45 mg

Spinach and Red Cabbage Salad with Oranges and Almonds

This colorful salad dresses up a plate, especially if the central dish is monochromatic. With spinach and oranges, it packs a lot of valuable vitamins. I recommend this salad frequently throughout the book.

4 TO 6 SERVINGS

4 to 6 ounces baby spinach
$1^1/2$ cups thinly shredded red cabbage
3 small seedless oranges, such as clementines, peeled and sectioned
$1/2$ medium cucumber, scrubbed, halved lengthwise, and thinly sliced
$1/4$ cup toasted slivered almonds
$1^1/2$ tablespoons extra virgin olive oil
$1^1/2$ tablespoons white balsamic or white wine vinegar, or to taste
Salt and freshly ground black pepper

Calories: 121
Total fat: 8 g
Protein: 3 g
Carbohydrates: 10 g
Fiber: 3 g
Sodium: 30 mg

1   Combine the spinach, cabbage, oranges, cucumber, and almonds in a serving bowl and toss together.

2   Dress as desired with oil and vinegar, then season to taste with salt and pepper. Toss again and serve.

Variation   This goes nicely with Asian-style dishes, and for use in those kinds of meals, consider replacing the olive oil and vinegar with Sesame-Ginger Salad Dressing (page 222) or its store-bought equivalent. You might also use a small head of radicchio in place of the cabbage.

Tri-Color Sweet and Tangy Peppers

This is an appetizing small side salad to serve when colorful bell peppers are plentiful. It goes well with pastas as well as grain dishes.

Combine all the ingredients in a serving bowl. Let stand for 10 to 15 minutes before serving.

4 TO 6 SERVINGS

1 large green bell pepper, cut into very thin 2-inch-long strips

1 large red bell pepper, cut to match green pepper

1 large yellow or orange bell pepper, cut to match green pepper

2 tablespoons extra virgin olive oil

3 tablespoons red wine vinegar

1 teaspoon natural granulated sugar

2 tablespoons minced fresh dill

Pinch of salt

Calories: 92
Total fat: 7 g
Protein: >1 g
Carbohydrates: 7 g
Fiber: 2 g
Sodium: 5 mg

Broccoli Salad with Yellow Peppers, Pine Nuts, and Cranberries

Luscious and yummy are rarely terms applied to salad, but I would be so bold as to use them to describe this one. Offbeat, colorful, and quick, it's a dish I make often in winter months when cool, crunchy salads are less enticing.

4 TO 6 SERVINGS

2 large broccoli crowns, cut into bite-size florets (about 4 heaping cups)

1 medium yellow bell pepper, diced

¼ cup pine nuts, lightly toasted in a dry skillet

⅓ cup dried cranberries

¼ cup Sesame-Ginger Salad Dressing (page 222) or equivalent store-bought dressing

Calories: 170
Total fat: 11 g
Protein: 5 g
Carbohydrates: 15 g
Fiber: 4 g
Sodium: 55 mg

1   Steam the broccoli florets just until bright green. Drain and rinse under cool water until room temperature or slightly warm.

2   Combine the broccoli and the remaining ingredients in a serving bowl, toss well, and serve.

Quinoa Tabouleh with Pine Nuts

Here's a nearly standard tabouleh recipe with a couple of interesting twists. Quinoa makes it fluffier and lighter than the traditional bulgur (not to mention even more nutritious), and pine nuts give it a rich flavor.

1   Combine the quinoa with 2¹/₂ cups water in a small saucepan. Bring to a simmer, then lower the heat. Cover and simmer gently for 15 minutes or until the water is absorbed.

2   Transfer the quinoa to a serving bowl and allow to cool to room temperature.

3   Add the remaining ingredients and toss gently until well combined. Serve at room temperature.

6 OR MORE SERVINGS

1¹/₄ cups quinoa, rinsed in a fine sieve

2 medium tomatoes, diced

¹/₂ cup halved yellow cherry or grape tomatoes

2 to 3 scallions, green parts only, thinly sliced

¹/₂ cup minced fresh parsley, or more, to taste

Juice of 1 lemon

2 tablespoons olive oil

Salt and freshly ground pepper to taste

¹/₃ cup pine nuts, lightly toasted in a dry skillet

Calories: 230
Total fat: 10 g
Protein: 7 g
Carbohydrates: 29 g
Fiber: 3 g
Sodium: 15 mg

Thai Tossed Salad

Inspired by the house salad I've enjoyed at Thai restaurants, this is the perfect companion to several of the Thai-style dishes in this book. A bigger portion of this can almost be the centerpiece of a meal, served with a simple tofu or tempeh dish.

6 SERVINGS

1 cup small broccoli florets, raw or lightly steamed

2 plum tomatoes, diced

$1/2$ medium cucumber, peeled and sliced

1 medium red bell pepper, cut into short, narrow strips

1 cup unsweetened pineapple chunks (about half of one 20-ounce can, drained)

1 large celery stalk, sliced diagonally

$1/2$ cup sliced cremini or baby bella mushrooms

Mixed baby greens, as desired

1 cup mung bean sprouts or $1/2$ cup green sprouts (such as sweet pea shoots)

$3/4$ cup Coconut-Peanut Sauce or Salad Dressing (page 215), or as needed

Calories: 91
Total fat: 3 g
Protein: 3 g
Carbohydrates: 13 g
Fiber: 3 g
Sodium: 85 mg

1   Combine all of the ingredients except the last three in a serving bowl.

2   To serve, arrange baby greens on a large serving platter. Top with the salad, then sprinkle with the sprouts. Serve, passing around the Coconut-Peanut Sauce for everyone to dress their salad as desired.

Black Beans with Tomatoes, Olives, Yellow Peppers, and Croutons

This appetizing bean salad adds color and crunch to a meal. Make it to bolster grain dishes and pastas.

Combine all the ingredients in a serving bowl and toss well. Let stand for 5 to 10 minutes before serving. Toss well again.

One 15- to 16-ounce can black beans, drained and rinsed
2 large or 4 medium tomatoes, diced
$1/2$ cup green pimiento-stuffed olives, halved
1 cup store-bought natural croutons
1 medium yellow bell pepper, cut into short, narrow strips
1 tablespoon extra virgin olive oil
1 tablespoon lemon or lime juice
2 tablespoons minced fresh dill
Freshly ground pepper to taste

Calories: 217
Total fat: 9.5 g
Protein: 8.5 g
Carbohydrates: 26.5 g
Fiber: 7 g
Sodium: 845 mg

SALADS AND VEGGIES ON THE SIDE

VEGAN EXPRESS

Black Bean, Mango, and Avocado Salad

In my part of the world (the Northeastern United States), we get the best mangos and avocados in mid- to late winter, just when our winter-weary palates need them most. This relishlike salad is not only scrumptious but also lovely to look at. It's especially welcome with Southwestern-style tortilla dishes.

6 SERVINGS

One 15- or 16-ounce can black beans, drained and rinsed

1 medium avocado, cut into ¼-inch dice

1 mango, cut into ¼-inch dice

½ red bell pepper, cut into ¼-inch dice

1 to 2 scallions, green parts only, thinly sliced

2 tablespoons extra virgin olive oil

2 tablespoons lime juice

Minced fresh cilantro to taste, optional

Calories: 174
Total fat: 10 g
Protein: 5 g
Carbohydrates: 18 g
Fiber: 6 g
Sodium: 175 mg

Combine all the ingredients in a serving bowl. Stir together and serve.

Salade Janine

Here is a salad I enjoyed on my first trip to Paris. It was part of a fantastic, produce-filled lunch in a private residence in Montmartre, overlooking much of the city. The key to this simple salad is to use the best possible ingredients—especially the green beans. Serve as a first course with slices of crusty, whole-grain baguette or Italian bread.

1 In a small heatproof container, pour $^1/_2$ cup boiling water over the couscous. Cover and let stand for 5 to 10 minutes, until the water is absorbed, then fluff with a fork.

2 Meanwhile, steam the green beans in a small amount of water until tender-crisp, then drain and rinse under cold water until cool.

3 Tear the lettuce into bite-size pieces. Combine the lettuce, avocado, tomatoes, and olives in a salad bowl. Gently stir in the couscous and green beans. Drizzle with vinaigrette, toss gently, and serve.

Note If really fresh, slender green beans are out of season, use organic frozen whole baby green beans, though the fresh version is much preferred in this salad. Steam the beans until tender-crisp to your liking, then refresh under cool water before adding to the salad.

4 TO 6 SERVINGS

$^1/_4$ cup couscous
2 cups (about $^1/_2$ pound) slender green beans (see Note)
1 large head Bibb or Boston lettuce
1 medium ripe, firm avocado, cut into thin strips
1 cup small grape tomatoes
$^1/_3$ cup small oil-cured black olives, preferably Niçoise
$^1/_4$ cup balsamic vinaigrette, homemade (page 221) or store-bought, or as needed

Calories: 277
Total fat: 21 g
Protein: 4 g
Carbohydrates: 20 g
Fiber: 5 g
Sodium: 275 mg

Sweet and White Potato Salad with Mixed Greens

One of the most fun things about traveling is finding food inspiration and ideas. I'm most drawn to simple preparations with creative twists. In Israel, I loved the myriad varieties of salads, which are served morning, noon, and night. I could spend a month in Israel just studying the salads.

On a recent trip, my family's last lunch before heading to the airport was at a lovely little café in the suburbs of Tel Aviv. One of the dishes we enjoyed was a mixture of sweet and white potatoes on a bed of greens. Nothing fancy, but it looked great and tasted even better. Once home, I made my copycat version of the salad, with two additions: a diced avocado mixed into the greens, and a topping of pumpkin seeds. It may look fancy, but it's very easy to make. The pleasing presentation makes it a good salad to impress company, as well as to bring to potlucks.

6 OR MORE SERVINGS

1 large sweet potato

4 medium white potatoes, preferably Yukon gold or red-skinned

1/2 cup vinaigrette, homemade (page 221) or store-bought

Salt and freshly ground pepper to taste

4 ounces mixed baby greens, or more as desired

1 cup cherry or grape tomatoes, halved

1 medium avocado, diced

Toasted pumpkin seeds

Calories: 277
Total fat: 18 g
Protein: 3 g
Carbohydrates: 28 g
Fiber: 4 g
Sodium: 70 mg

1   Microwave the sweet and white potatoes separately until done but still nice and firm. Start with 3 minutes, then test. When done, plunge into a bowl of cold water.

2   When the potatoes are cool enough to handle, peel and dice them. Combine in a mixing bowl with half of the vinaigrette; season with salt and pepper.

3   Line a large serving platter with the greens. Mound the potato mixture in the center.

4   Scatter the tomatoes and avocado around the perimeter of the salad. Top the potato mixture with a sprinkling of pumpkin seeds. Serve at once, passing additional vinaigrette.

Cauliflower and Carrot Salad

Here's a salad with plenty of personality. I like to make this as part of a meal of cool dishes in the summer, either with a cold soup or with two additional interesting salads.

1   Place the cauliflower in a skillet with a small amount of water. Cover and steam for 2 minutes, then add the carrots. Continue to steam, covered, until both are tender-crisp, 2 to 3 minutes longer.

2   Transfer the vegetables to a colander and refresh under cool water.

3   Combine the cauliflower and carrots in a serving bowl with the remaining ingredients. Toss well. Serve at once.

4 TO 6 SERVINGS

1 small head cauliflower, cut into bite-size florets

1 cup baby carrots, halved lengthwise

1/2 cup pitted black olives, preferably oil-cured

1/4 cup minced fresh parsley or cilantro, or more to taste

2 scallions, green parts only, thinly sliced

1/4 cup vinaigrette, homemade (page 221) or store-bought, or as needed to moisten

Salt and freshly ground pepper to taste

Calories: 217
Total fat: 16 g
Protein: 3 g
Carbohydrates: 13 g
Fiber: 4 g
Sodium: 425 mg

Chickpea and Carrot Salad with Parsley and Olives

This adaptation of a traditional Middle Eastern salad is filled with vigorous flavors and textures. I especially like it with Middle Eastern- or Spanish-themed meals. For a light summer meal, serve this with Sweet and White Potato Salad with Mixed Greens (page 188).

4 TO 6 SERVINGS

One 15- to 16-ounce can chickpeas, drained and rinsed

1 cup packed grated carrots (see Note)

1/2 cup minced fresh parsley

2 to 3 scallions, green parts only, thinly sliced

1/2 cup chopped green pimiento-stuffed olives

Juice of 1/2 to 1 lemon, to taste

2 tablespoons extra virgin olive oil

1/2 teaspoon ground cumin

Salt and freshly ground pepper to taste

Calories: 210
Total fat: 12 g
Protein: 5 g
Carbohydrates: 21 g
Fiber: 7 g
Sodium: 800 mg

Combine the ingredients in a serving container. Toss well, then serve.

Note   For greater ease, use baby carrots, eliminating the need to peel and cut before grating. Even easier is using pregrated carrots, but make sure they're fresh and not dried out.

Middle Eastern Chopped Salad

This wonderful salad is a perfect accompaniment to classic Middle Eastern dishes. You can also build a meal around it in the summertime; serve with store-bought or homemade hummus, fresh pita bread, and stuffed grape leaves. See the menu with Tofu Shakshouka (page 45) for another menu idea. Make sure to use an organic, unwaxed cucumber, as it's best unpeeled in this salad.

Combine all the ingredients in a serving bowl and toss together. If time allows, let the salad stand for 10 minutes or so to allow the flavors to blend.

4 TO 6 SERVINGS

3 medium tomatoes, diced

1 medium cucumber, scrubbed and diced

1 yellow or orange bell pepper, diced

$1/3$ cup pitted black olives, preferably oil-cured

2 scallions, thinly sliced, or $1/4$ cup quartered and thinly sliced red onion

$1/4$ cup minced fresh parsley

2 tablespoons extra virgin olive oil

Juice of 1 lemon

2 teaspoons sesame seeds

$1/4$ cup toasted pine nuts, optional

Salt and freshly ground pepper to taste

Calories: 165
Total fat: 12 g
Protein: 2 g
Carbohydrates: 12 g
Fiber: 3.5 g
Sodium: 220 mg

RECIPE NOT REQUIRED *To Make Dazzling Green Salads*

If I were to name "the best thing since sliced bread," I'd have to say mixed baby greens. Where once they used to seem precious, even pretentious, now they are a staple of supermarket greens sections; even my CSA (community-supported agriculture) farm supplies them (and are they ever fantastic when freshly harvested!). When the greens supply such a lovely palette of colors and variety of textures, just a few additional ingredients are needed to create a spectacular salad. Here are a few favorites of mine; feel free to mix and match, as well as to create your own signature salads starring mixed greens.

Start with mixed baby greens (to which you can add extra arugula or baby spinach, if you like), then add:

• Strips of sun-dried tomatoes, diced fresh tomatoes, thinly sliced yellow or orange bell pepper, sliced cucumber, toasted pine nuts or sunflower seeds

• Artichoke hearts (marinated or not, as you prefer), pan-roasted corn kernels, cherry or grape tomatoes, toasted sunflower or pumpkin seeds

• Diced Asian pear, sweet pea shoots or other sprouts, chopped toasted cashews, pickled beets

• Diced apple, pear, or Asian pear; diced avocado; red bell pepper; toasted walnuts or pecans (optional: add a tiny head of radicchio)

• Diced Granny Smith apple; avocado; sliced carrots or baby carrots; toasted walnuts, pecans, or pumpkin seeds

• Sliced pickled beets, sliced crisp cucumber, diced daikon radish or turnip, fresh dill and/or cilantro

• Sliced red pepper, cured black olives, yellow grape tomatoes, sliced brown mushrooms (raw or steamed)

• Sliced mushrooms; matchstick-cut baby carrots; sliced bok choy and white turnip, daikon radish, or Jerusalem artichoke; Sesame-Ginger Salad Dressing (homemade, page 222, or store-bought)

My favorite way of dressing these pretty salads is with a little olive or flaxseed oil and lemon juice, but you may dress them in whatever way you prefer. Some of the fruity salads, for instance, taste good with French dressing or raspberry vinaigrette.

Warm Mediterranean Potato Salad

This flavorful warm salad can be made any time of year, its seasonal personality lent by either rosemary (for cooler months) or basil (for warmer weather). It's a fairly substantial salad, so it's good served with a straightforward protein dish like Tempeh Fries (page 78), Cornmeal-Crusted Seitan (page 63), or BBQ-Flavored Skillet Tofu (page 62).

6 SERVINGS

1   Scrub the potatoes well and microwave them in their skins until done but still firm, about 2 minutes per potato. Plunge into a bowl of ice water.

2   Halve the zucchini lengthwise, then slice thinly. Combine in a serving bowl with the fennel, artichoke hearts, and sun-dried tomatoes.

3   When the potatoes are just cool enough to handle, cut them into large dice and stir into the serving bowl. Add the fresh herbs and optional pine nuts.

4   Stir gently, then season with lemon juice to taste, salt, and pepper. Serve at once.

4 to 5 large red-skinned potatoes
2 small zucchini
1/2 cup sliced fennel or diced celery
One 6-ounce jar marinated artichoke hearts, undrained
1/4 cup oil-packed sun-dried tomatoes, cut into strips, with about 2 tablespoons of their oil
Leaves from 1 to 2 sprigs fresh rosemary, or more to taste, or sliced fresh basil leaves as desired
2 tablespoons toasted pine nuts, optional
2 to 3 tablespoons lemon juice
Salt and freshly ground pepper to taste

Calories: 205
Total fat: 8 g
Protein: 4 g
Carbohydrates: 31 g
Fiber: 5 g
Sodium: 190 mg

Fingerling Fries

Here's a quick and clever way to make potato fries without a lot of peeling and cutting. Fingerling potatoes, if you are not familiar with them, are small potatoes with a long, narrow shape—hence their name. They come in several varieties; I like to use organic golden fingerlings like Russian Banana. These are ready, from start to finish, in about 20 minutes.

4 TO 6 SERVINGS

1½ pounds fingerling potatoes
2 tablespoons light or extra virgin olive oil
Salt to taste
Paprika to taste (see Note)

Calories: 145
Total fat: 3 g
Protein: 4 g
Carbohydrates: 30 g
Fiber: 3 g
Sodium: 0 mg

1   Scrub the potatoes well. No need to peel them, but do cut away any overly dark or knobby spots, of which there should be few. Cut each potato in half lengthwise, which results in a short, chunky French-fry shape.

2   Place the potatoes in a nonstick skillet with ½ cup water. Bring to a simmer, then lower the heat and cover. Simmer steadily for 5 to 8 minutes, stirring occasionally, or until the potatoes can be pierced with a knife but are still quite firm. Drain any water from the skillet.

3   Drizzle in the olive oil. Turn the heat to medium-high and fry the potatoes, stirring frequently, until touched with golden brown on most sides, 5 to 8 minutes.

4   Remove from the heat and season with salt and paprika.

Note   If you'd like a more exotic effect, try Spanish paprika, which has a smoky and more intense flavor than Hungarian sweet paprika.

Rosemary Roasted Potatoes with Black Olives

You can almost build a meal around this simple, delicious side dish. Once you've got the potatoes in the oven you have plenty of time to make a bountiful salad. You can also put Teriyaki Tofu Steaks (page 62) or store-bought veggie burgers in the oven at the same time for a no-fuss "meat and potatoes" kind of meal.

1   Preheat the oven to 425°F.

2   Scrub the potatoes well, then cut into quarters.

3   Use a small amount of the light olive oil to oil the roasting pan (or line the pan with baking parchment for easy clean-up). In a large mixing bowl, toss the potatoes with the remaining light olive oil. Arrange in a single layer in the pan.

4   Roast for 15 minutes, then stir and sprinkle on the rosemary and olives. Bake for 10 to 15 minutes longer, until the outsides of the potatoes are golden and the insides tender.

5   Transfer the potatoes to a serving bowl and drizzle with the extra virgin olive oil. Toss to coat, season with salt and pepper, and serve.

6 SERVINGS

2 pounds small Yukon gold or red-skinned potatoes
2 tablespoons light olive oil
Leaves from 2 to 3 sprigs fresh rosemary, or more to taste
⅓ cup pitted oil-cured black olives
1 tablespoon extra virgin olive oil
Salt and freshly ground pepper to taste

Calories: 206
Total fat: 10 g
Protein: 4 g
Carbohydrates: 28 g
Fiber: 3 g
Sodium: 185 mg

Spanish Bell Pepper Sauté

Summer is the prefect time to make the luscious Spanish classic, piperade, when peppers of all colors are abundant and, for a short time, relatively inexpensive. This is a great partner for almost any sort of pasta or grain dish, hot or cold, or to serve alongside a summertime sandwich. Use leftovers in wraps.

4 TO 6 SERVINGS

2 tablespoons olive oil

1 medium onion, quartered and thinly sliced

2 garlic cloves, minced

2 medium red bell peppers, cut into narrow strips

2 medium green bell peppers, cut to match red pepper

2 medium yellow bell peppers, cut to match red pepper

1/4 cup dry white wine

1/4 cup oil-packed sun-dried tomatoes, cut into strips

2 medium tomatoes

2 to 3 tablespoons minced fresh parsley, optional

Salt and freshly ground pepper to taste

Calories: 150
Total fat: 9 g
Protein: 2 g
Carbohydrates: 15 g
Fiber: 4 g
Sodium: 50 mg

1   Heat the oil in a large skillet. Add the onion and sauté over medium heat until translucent.

2   Add the garlic, bell peppers, wine, and sun-dried tomatoes. Stir in 1/4 cup water and bring to a simmer. Cook, covered, over medium-low heat until the peppers are tender but not overdone, about 8 minutes.

3   Stir in the fresh tomatoes and continue to cook, uncovered, just until they have lost their raw quality, 3 to 4 minutes. Add the optional parsley and season with salt and pepper. Serve at once.

Spicy Sesame Broccoli

Broccoli is given a spark of heat in this speedy preparation. This is a good way to complement Asian-style rice, noodle, or tofu dishes.

1   Cut the broccoli crowns into bite-size florets.

2   Gently heat the soy sauce, oil, and wine in a medium skillet. Stir in the sugar. Add the broccoli and stir quickly to coat. Turn the heat to medium high and cover.

3   Steam until the broccoli is bright green and just tender-crisp, about 3 minutes. Uncover and stir-fry until any liquid remaining in the skillet is reduced. Stir in the sesame seeds, season with red pepper flakes to taste, and serve.

SERVES 4

2 large or 3 medium broccoli crowns
*1 tablespoon reduced-sodium soy
    sauce*
1 tablespoon dark sesame oil
2 tablespoons white wine or water
1 tablespoon natural granulated sugar
2 teaspoons sesame seeds
Dried red pepper flakes

Calories: 90
Total fat: 4.5 g
Protein: 4 g
Carbohydrates: 10 g
Fiber: 3.5 g
Sodium: 165 mg

Sautéed Cauliflower with Sun-Dried Tomatoes and Basil

In our home, cauliflower is a favorite vegetable, second only to broccoli. We're more than glad to have it steamed, with just a splash of flaxseed oil, but the combination of dried tomatoes and basil adds a special touch.

6 SERVINGS

1 medium or large head cauliflower, cut into bite-size pieces
1 tablespoon extra virgin olive oil
1/3 cup oil-packed sliced sun-dried tomatoes
Salt and freshly ground pepper to taste
Sliced fresh basil leaves, optional

Calories: 78
Total fat: 4 g
Protein: 2 g
Carbohydrates: 9 g
Fiber: 3 g
Sodium: 70 mg

1   Combine the cauliflower with $1/2$ cup water in a large skillet or stir-fry pan. Cover and steam over medium heat until tender but still firm, about 8 minutes.

2   Drain any water from the pan, then drizzle in the olive oil. Stir in the sun-dried tomatoes and cook for 2 to 3 minutes longer. Season with salt and pepper, top with basil if desired, and serve.

Pan-Roasted Corn with Red Peppers and Pumpkin Seeds

Here's my favorite way to dress up frozen corn kernels. Not surprising, it's even better with fresh corn, as described in the variation. Serve this as a side dish to Southwestern-style specialties and bean dishes.

1   In a wide skillet, combine the corn kernels and about $1/4$ cup water. Cover and cook for 3 to 4 minutes, until the kernels are tender-crisp. Drain the water.

2   Drizzle in the oil, then stir in the bell pepper, optional chile pepper, and pumpkin seeds. Turn the heat to medium high and cook, stirring frequently, until the corn kernels are touched here and there with browned spots.

3   Season with cumin, salt, and pepper and serve.

Variation   If you have more time, make this with fresh corn. Use 4 large ears of fresh sweet corn. Holding the ears of corn upright on their flat ends (one at a time, of course), remove the kernels with a sharp knife.

6 SERVINGS

One 16-ounce bag frozen corn kernels, thawed

1 tablespoon olive oil

1 medium red bell pepper, cut into narrow 2-inch strips

1 small jalapeño or other hot chile pepper, seeded and minced, optional

$1/4$ cup roasted pumpkin seeds

Pinch of ground cumin

Salt and freshly ground pepper to taste

Calories: 144
Total fat: 7 g
Protein: 6 g
Carbohydrates: 19 g
Fiber: 7 g
Sodium: 5 mg

Zucchini and Polenta Marinara

This dish is almost embarrassingly easy, but such a crowd-pleaser that I just had to share it. Use a flavorful prepared marinara—smoked tomato, mushroom, or chunky vegetable.

6 SERVINGS

One 18-ounce tube polenta
2 medium zucchini, sliced $1/4$ inch thick
One 28-ounce jar good-quality marinara sauce
$1^1/2$ cups grated vegan mozzarella cheese
Sliced fresh basil leaves, optional

Calories: 257
Total fat: 14 g
Protein: 6 g
Carbohydrates: 26g
Fiber: 6 g
Sodium: 920 mg

1 Preheat the oven to 425°F.

2 Cut the polenta into $1/2$-inch-thick slices. Spread a little of the marinara sauce over the bottom of a shallow $1^1/2$-quart baking dish. Arrange the polenta slices in a single layer.

3 Arrange the zucchini slices over the polenta, then pour the remaining sauce evenly over them.

4 Sprinkle the surface evenly with the cheese. Cover and bake for 10 minutes, then uncover and bake for 5 to 10 minutes longer, until the cheese is melted and bubbly. Serve at once, garnishing each serving with fresh basil if desired.

Garlicky Greens

You may not feel like dealing with a big mess o' greens when you're in a huge hurry to eat, but if your main dish is a breeze and you have a few minutes to spare, it's a great investment of time. Recently, I fell in love with kale, so preparing a batch in this manner no longer seems like a big deal. Greens—especially kale and collards—provide a reliable source of calcium for vegans. This is a good way to prepare Swiss chard, kale, or collard greens.

1   Remove the stems and thick ribs from the greens. Especially if using kale or collards, wash the leaves thoroughly, a small batch at a time, in a large colander or bowl.

2   Heat the oil in a large soup pot or stir-fry pan. Add the garlic and sauté over low heat for 2 to 3 minutes, until golden.

3   Add the greens with water as needed, cover, and steam until just tender. For Swiss chard, the water clinging to the leaves after rinsing is sufficient for steaming. For kale, collards, and other hearty greens, add $1/4$ to $1/2$ cup water, as needed. Steaming time varies greatly from one type of green to another, so check frequently. Swiss chard takes 3 to 5 minutes; kale and collards may need 10 to 15 minutes.

4   When the greens are done, drain in a colander. Discard the garlic cloves. Press out some of the liquid, then transfer to a cutting board and chop coarsely.

5   Transfer the greens to a serving dish and toss with the lemon juice. Season with salt and pepper and serve at once.

4 TO 6 SERVINGS

1 large bunch (about 1 pound) greens of your choice
1 tablespoon extra virgin olive oil
3 to 4 garlic cloves, crushed
2 tablespoons lemon juice, or to taste
Salt and freshly ground pepper to taste

Calories: 93
Total fat: 4 g
Protein: 4 g
Carbohydrates: 13 g
Fiber: 4 g
Sodium: 50 mg

Mediterranean Spinach with Pine Nuts and Raisins

This classic recipe is a good way to highlight this nourishing green vegetable. The rich flavor of pine nuts and sweetness of raisins are surprising yet compatible in tandem with the spinach.

4 SERVINGS

1 tablespoon extra virgin olive oil
2 garlic cloves, crushed
2 to 3 tablespoons pine nuts
10 to 12 ounces baby spinach
1 tablespoon lemon juice
1/4 cup raisins
Salt and freshly ground pepper to taste

Calories: 100
Total fat: 6 g
Protein: 3 g
Carbohydrates: 11 g
Fiber: 3 g
Sodium: 60 mg

1   Heat the oil in a soup pot or stir-fry pan. Add the garlic and sauté over low heat for 1 minute, stirring frequently. Add pine nuts to taste and continue to sauté, stirring often, until the nuts and garlic are golden, about 3 minutes longer.

2   Add the spinach and cover. Cook for just a minute or two, until the spinach is wilted but still bright green. Remove from the heat.

3   Stir in the lemon juice and raisins, season with salt and pepper, and serve.

This is not, by any means, a comprehensive survey of vegetables, nor an exhaustive list of what you can do with them. This list briefly details my personal favorite ways to prepare common veggies—flash-in-the-pan side dishes that enhance the already wonderful flavor of organic vegetables, and for which a formal recipe is not necessary. Use what you've got and make as much as you need, keeping this list handy as a template for ideas for making easy accompaniments. To avoid redundancy, I haven't listed salt and pepper; assume that you can season any of the following dishes with salt and pepper to taste.

Asparagus

SAUTÉED ASPARAGUS WITH ALMONDS: For speed and ease, use slender asparagus spears that need no peeling if possible; otherwise, scrape the bottom halves of the spears. In either case, trim off about an inch from the bottoms. Cut the spears in half or into thirds. Heat enough olive oil to coat a skillet; add the asparagus and a sprinkling of slivered or sliced almonds. Sauté over medium heat until the asparagus is tender-crisp about 3 to 5 minutes depending on thickness.

ROASTED ASPARAGUS WITH SESAME SEEDS AND SESAME OIL: Preheat the oven or toaster oven to 400°F. For roasting, I prefer medium rather than slender spears so they don't dwindle to nothing. Trim about an inch from the bottoms, then peel the bottom halves of the spears. Arrange the spears on a lightly oiled baking pan and drizzle with sesame oil. Sprinkle with sesame seeds. Roast until tender and lightly browned, stirring occasionally, 10 to 15 minutes.

MY FAVORITE SIMPLE VEGETABLE SIDE DISHES, FROM ASPARAGUS TO ZUCCHINI

Bell Peppers

BELL PEPPER AND BOK CHOY STIR-FRY: Cut 1 or 2 bell peppers (any color) into long, narrow strips. In a stir-fry pan or large skillet, heat light olive oil with a little soy sauce. Stir-fry the peppers together with 4 to 6 good-sized stalks of sliced bok choy, with greens, over medium-high heat for 3 minutes or so. To vary this recipe, add a cup or so of sliced mushrooms or a handful of chopped cashews.

See also Spanish Bell Pepper Sauté (page 196).

Broccoli

STEAMED BROCCOLI WITH CAULIFLOWER: I often steam these two cruciferous veggies together, especially when I have just one crown of broccoli and half of a cauliflower left in the fridge. To finish, drizzle with a little flaxseed oil.

BROCCOLI WITH MUSTARD-SPIKED CHEESE SAUCE: Steam a big batch of broccoli florets until tender-crisp, pass around the sauce (page 212), and watch the broccoli disappear quickly!

BROCCOLI WITH PINE NUTS OR ALMONDS: Toss steamed broccoli florets with a little olive oil or flaxseed oil and add a sprinkling of lightly toasted pine nuts.

See also Spicy Sesame Broccoli (page 197).

Brussels Sprouts

STEAMED BRUSSELS SPROUTS WITH SUNFLOWER SEEDS: Don't ask me why, but I just love the way sunflower seeds enhance the flavor of this underappreciated vegetable. Trim the stem ends from about a pint of Brussels sprouts, cut them in half, and steam just until they are bright green and tender to your liking, about 3 to 5 minutes. Please don't overcook them! Drain, toss with a little flaxseed or olive oil, and sprinkle with about 3 tablespoons of toasted sunflower seeds.

ROASTED BRUSSELS SPROUTS: Preheat the oven to 425°F. Trim the stem ends from about a pint of Brussels sprouts, cut them in half, and toss with olive oil. Sprinkle with salt-free seasoning such as Spike or Mrs. Dash, if you like. Roast for about 20 minutes, or until lightly browned. Vary this by adding 2 cups of baby carrots for a larger and more colorful vegetable dish.

Cabbage (Green)

SAUTÉED CABBAGE AND ONIONS: I find that when I buy a good-sized green cabbage and use a small amount in a recipe, the remainder often languishes in the fridge. This is an ideal way to use up green cabbage while it still has some flavor. For this preparation, you can use half or even most of a cabbage. In a large skillet or stir-fry pan, sauté a quartered and thinly sliced onion in some olive oil. When it starts to turn golden, stir in thinly sliced cabbage. Cook, covered, until the cabbage wilts. If the pan dries out, add just enough water to moisten. Once the cabbage is wilted, uncover and cook until both the cabbage and onion begin to brown, stirring frequently. Add a sprinkling of poppy seeds, if you like.

Carrots

MAPLE-ROASTED BABY CARROTS: Combine a 16-ounce bag of baby carrots with maple syrup to taste, a little light olive oil, and cinnamon; toss, and roast in a 425°F oven for about 20 minutes, or until tender. Additionally, you can stir some chopped walnuts or pecans into the mix.

STIR-FRIED BABY CARROTS: Combine carrots in a skillet or stir-fry pan with a little water. Cover and steam for 10 minutes, or until they are just starting to turn tender-crisp. Drain the water and drizzle in a little light olive oil. Add another ingredient or ingredients or your choice: chopped dried fruit, chopped nuts, baby corn, green peas, and so forth. Stir-fry until the carrots are tender-crisp and beginning to turn golden.

Cauliflower

CAULIFLOWER WITH BREAD CRUMBS: Whirl 1 or 2 slices of bread in a food processor until reduced to crumbs. Heat a little nonhydrogenated margarine in a small skillet, add the crumbs, and toast over medium heat until golden, about 5 minutes. Set aside. Cut a medium head of cauliflower into bite-size pieces. Combine in a large skillet or stir-fry pan with about ¹⁄₂ cup water. Cover and steam over medium heat until tender but still firm, about 8 minutes. Stir occasionally. Drain any water remaining in the pan. Stir in the bread crumbs and sprinkle with a little paprika.

See also Steamed Broccoli with Cauliflower (page 204) and Sautéed Cauliflower with Sun-Dried Tomatoes and Basil (page 198).

Corn

CORN WITH EDAMAME: I think of this combination as a contemporary succotash (the traditional version uses lima beans, which don't quite have the personality of edamame). Combine cooked corn kernels with cooked shelled edamame (I like to use a proportion of 2 parts corn to 1 part edamame). Stir in a little nonhydrogenated margarine, olive oil, or flaxseed oil if you like; you can also embellish this dish with scallions or chives.

See also Pan-Roasted Corn with Red Peppers and Pumpkin Seeds (page 199).

Green Beans

GREEN BEANS TERIYAKI: Fresh slender green beans work best for this, but if you're in a hurry, use frozen organic whole baby green beans, completely thawed. Heat a little oil, prepared teriyaki sauce, and a pinch of natural granulated sugar in a stir-fry pan, add the green beans, and stir-fry over medium-high heat until nicely browned. If you like, rev up the flavor with chopped garlic, ginger, and/or fresh chile pepper.

GREEN BEANS CREOLE: Sauté a little minced garlic in a medium skillet until golden; add green beans and a little water; steam just until bright green. Drain the water and add 1 or 2 chopped tomatoes, plus fresh basil leaves and lemon juice to taste. Cover and cook until the tomatoes have softened and the green beans are done to your liking.

Potatoes

SAUTÉED PAPRIKA POTATOES: Microwave potatoes until done but still firm. Plunge into a bowl of ice water. When cool enough to handle, peel and slice. Sauté in a small amount of olive oil. When the potatoes begin to turn golden, add lots of sliced scallions and a generous sprinkling of paprika (use smoky Spanish paprika if you like; see Note on page 194). Continue to sauté until the potatoes brown lightly. Add some minced garlic along with the scallions if you're a garlic fan.

SMASHED YUKON GOLD POTATOES WITH SHIITAKE-MISO GRAVY:
Simply bake or microwave as many good-size Yukon gold
potatoes as you need (allowing one whole or half potato per
serving), until tender. Leaving them in their jackets, cut each
potato in half, smash lightly with a potato masher, and serve hot
with freshly made Shiitake-Miso Gravy (page 217).

See also Fingerling Fries (page 194) and Rosemary Roasted
Potatoes with Black Olives (page 195).

Spinach

SESAME SPINACH: Use at least 10 to 12 ounces (a pound is even
better) of fresh spinach or, for easier preparation, baby spinach.
Rinse the spinach (and in the case of regular spinach, trim any
large stems). Wilt the leaves in a skillet or stir-fry pan for a
minute or so, then stir in a little sesame oil, soy sauce, and a
sprinkling of sesame seeds.

See also Mediterranean Spinach with Pine Nuts and Raisins
(page 202).

Sweet Potatoes

I consider sweet potatoes to be one of the crown jewels of the
vegetable world, and though I use them often in cooking
(especially in soups and stews, and in roasted vegetable
mélanges), adding much embellishment to them as a side dish is
gilding the lily. I often simply microwave them in their jackets
until tender, split them in half, and moisten with a little
nonhydrogenated margarine.

Prepping and roasting sweet potatoes takes a bit more time
than you might want to spend when preparing speedy meals, but
when you do have time, roasting them (either alone, with other
root vegetables, or with apples) is an ideal way to enhance their

flavor. Otherwise, the following are delightful ways to serve them.

SMASHED SWEET POTATOES WITH CASHEW BUTTER SAUCE: Use as many medium to large sweet potatoes as you need, allowing one whole or half sweet potato per serving. To bake, preheat the oven to 375°F. Wrap each potato in foil and place on the oven rack; bake for about 40 minutes, or until easily pierced with a knife. To microwave, allow 2 minutes per medium potato and 3 minutes per large. Test with a knife; if still too firm, cook an additional 1 minute per potato until done.

Leaving the sweet potatoes in their jackets, cut each in half, smash lightly with a potato masher, and serve hot with freshly made Cashew Butter Sauce (page 216).

SMASHED SWEET POTATOES WITH INSTANT ROASTED RED PEPPER SAUCE: Use the same directions as in the preceding suggestion, but serve with Instant Roasted Red Pepper Sauce (page 220) instead.

Zucchini and/or Yellow Summer Squash

ZUCCHINI AND SUMMER SQUASH SAUTÉ: For an easy side dish, I like to combine zucchini and yellow summer squash, cut into approximately 3-inch spears, and sauté them in olive oil with garlic until golden. For extra flavor, add a sprinkling of ground cumin and/or sliced basil leaves.

See also Zucchini and Polenta Marinara, page 200.

CHAPTER EIGHT

Sauces and Salad Dressings

This chapter contains a concise collection of sauces and dressings used in some of the recipes in this book. I put them in their own section, as I'd like to encourage you to consider using them as you please, mixing and matching with other recipes in these pages or in preparations of your own. Most of these recipes take minutes to prepare, and since most of the ingredients are pantry staples, the makings of a great dressing or sauce should always be at hand.

I'm not at all opposed to using prepared dressings and sauces; in fact, I'm a great proponent of such shortcuts. Given a limited amount of time, I almost always opt for cutting up lots of vegetables over preparing a sauce. But sometimes you just can't beat the freshness and creativity of a homemade sauce or dressing. I've given only a couple of standard recipes here (Basic Vinaigrette and Sesame-Ginger Salad Dressing); the others are offbeat preparations that won't be found in a store. When you're looking for ways to dress up vegetables, tofu, grains, potatoes, noodles, and tortilla specialties, this chapter offers a brief but useful selection.

Mustard-Spiked Cheese Sauce

This luscious sauce makes vegetables (broccoli, cauliflower, green beans, Brussels sprouts) more appealing to the finicky, but even veggie lovers will enjoy this cheesy treat.

MAKES ABOUT 2 CUPS

3/4 cup silken tofu (about half of a 12.3-ounce package)

1/4 cup rice milk, plus more as needed

1 tablespoon nonhydrogenated margarine

1 1/2 cups firmly packed grated vegan Cheddar cheese

2 teaspoons prepared mustard (yellow or Dijon-style, as you prefer), or more to taste

1/2 teaspoon dry mustard

1/2 teaspoon paprika

Salt to taste

PER 1/4 CUP
Calories: 97
Total fat: 9 g
Protein: 2 g
Carbohydrates: 3 g
Fiber: 2 g
Sodium: 185 mg

1   Puree the tofu with the rice milk in a food processor or the container of an immersion blender.

2   Transfer to a small saucepan and add the remaining ingredients except the salt. Bring to a gentle simmer over medium heat and cook, stirring frequently, until the cheese has melted, about 5 minutes. Add a bit more rice milk if desired to make the sauce more fluid. You can also use an immersion blender in the pot to make the sauce more velvety.

3   Season with salt (you may not need much, if any) and serve hot over steamed vegetables.

Vegan Sour Cream

Here's an easy preparation that's quite useful since vegan sour cream is not yet a common product in stores. I especially like this as a garnish for Southwestern-style dishes like Tortilla Casserole (page 104) and cold soups like Cool White Bean and Cucumber Soup (page 38).

Combine all the ingredients in a food processor or the companion container to an immersion blender. Process until very smoothly pureed, then transfer to a container with an airtight lid.

MAKES A LITTLE MORE THAN 1 CUP

1 cup crumbled firm or extra-firm silken tofu

2 to 3 tablespoons rice milk or Silk creamer, as needed

2 teaspoons lemon juice, or more to taste

$1/4$ teaspoon salt, or to taste

PER $1/4$ CUP
Calories: 21
Total fat: 1 g
Protein: 2 g
Carbohydrates: 1 g
Fiber: 0 g
Sodium: 88 mg

Rich Peanut Sauce

In creating this recipe, I tried to reproduce the flavors in a peanut sauce that was served over skewers of tofu in an Indonesian restaurant my sons and I visited in Amsterdam. I'm sure this is a simplified rendition, but no matter—it's really good! Use it to top sautéed tofu or tempeh; it's also good with noodles. See Golden Tofu Triangles with Rich Peanut Sauce (page 46).

MAKES ABOUT 1^1/$_2$ CUPS

^{3}/$_4$ cup crunchy natural peanut butter

3 tablespoons reduced-sodium soy sauce

2^1/$_2$ tablespoons lime juice

2 tablespoons natural granulated sugar

2 teaspoons grated fresh ginger

^{1}/$_2$ to 1 teaspoon Thai red curry paste, to taste

PER ^{1}/$_4$ CUP
Calories: 210
Total fat: 16 g
Protein: 8 g
Carbohydrates: 12 g
Fiber: 2 g
Sodium: 285 mg

1   Combine all the ingredients in a small saucepan with ^{1}/$_2$ cup water. Whisk together and heat to a gentle simmer.

2   Cook over low heat for 2 minutes, stirring frequently. Add a bit more water if too thick. Serve warm or at room temperature over tofu, tempeh, or Asian noodle dishes.

Coconut-Peanut Sauce or Salad Dressing

This luscious mixture is as welcome on raw salads as it is over cooked noodle, grain, or vegetable dishes.

1   Combine the ingredients in a small mixing bowl and whisk together until completely combined. Use at room temperature as a dressing.

2   If you'd like to use this as a warm sauce, combine the ingredients in a small saucepan, whisk together, and heat gently until warm.

MAKES ABOUT 1½ CUPS

One 8-ounce jar Thai peanut satay sauce
½ cup light coconut milk
Juice of 1 lime
½ teaspoon red or green Thai chile paste, or to taste, dissolved in a little hot water
2 teaspoons brown rice syrup, agave nectar, or maple syrup

PER ¼ CUP
Calories: 97
Total fat: 6 g
Protein: 1 g
Carbohydrates: 8 g
Fiber: 1 g
Sodium: 135 mg

Cashew Butter Sauce

A version of this sauce appeared in my first book, *Vegetariana,* and I've used it ever since. It's one of the most luscious, versatile sauces in my repertoire—it tastes great on sweet potatoes (see Smashed Sweet Potatoes with Cashew Butter Sauce, page 209), mashed potatoes, grains, vegetables, and noodles.

MAKES ABOUT 2 CUPS

2 teaspoons olive oil

1/2 medium red, orange, or yellow bell pepper, finely diced

2 to 3 scallions, minced

1 cup finely diced tomato

1 tablespoon unbleached white flour

1 cup vegetable stock or water

1/2 cup cashew butter

1/2 teaspoon good-quality curry powder

1/2 teaspoon minced fresh ginger, optional

Salt and freshly ground pepper to taste

PER 1/4 CUP
Calories: 116
Total fat: 9 g
Protein: 3 g
Carbohydrates: 7 g
Fiber: 1 g
Sodium: 50 mg

1 Heat the oil in a saucepan. Add the bell pepper and scallions and cook over medium-low heat until the pepper softens, about 4 minutes.

2 Add the tomato and cook for 3 to 4 minutes longer, stirring, until it softens.

3 Sprinkle in the flour and stir until well blended with the vegetables. Pour in the stock and bring to a gentle simmer.

4 Whisk in the cashew butter, then add the curry and optional ginger. Cook for another 2 to 3 minutes, until smooth and thick. Season with salt and pepper. Serve at once or cover until needed, then heat through before serving.

Shiitake-Miso Gravy

Serve this versatile sauce to dress up sautéed tofu, tempeh, or mashed potatoes. See suggestions for its use in Smashed Yukon Gold Potatoes with Shiitake-Miso Gravy (page 208) and Tempeh and Green Beans with Shiitake-Miso Gravy (page 76).

1   Combine the broth, mushrooms, ginger to taste, and oil in a small saucepan. Bring to a rapid simmer, then cover and simmer gently for 5 to 7 minutes.

2   In a small container, combine the cornstarch with just enough water to dissolve. Whisk it into the saucepan and cook just until the gravy thickens. Remove from the heat.

3   Combine the miso with $^{1}/_{4}$ cup warm water in a small bowl and whisk until smooth. Stir into the gravy. Season with pepper to taste and serve at once, or cover and heat through just before serving.

Note   You can use your favorite variety of miso (including dark, pungent barley or hatcho); my personal preference here is for mellow white miso.

MAKES ABOUT 2 CUPS

1 cup vegetable broth or water
2 cups thinly sliced shiitake mushroom caps (2 to 3 ounces)
1 to 2 teaspoons minced fresh ginger
1 teaspoon dark sesame oil
1$^{1}/_{2}$ tablespoons cornstarch
2 rounded tablespoons miso (see Note)
Freshly ground pepper

PER $^{1}/_{4}$ CUP
Calories: 29
Total fat: 1 g
Protein: 1 g
Carbohydrates: 3 g
Fiber: 0 g
Sodium: 280 mg

Easy Gravy

This gravy was inspired by my family's visit to Taste of Life, a wonderful vegan eatery in Tel Aviv. The café is run by the community of Black Hebrews, who also produce most of the tofu and seitan distributed in Israel at their village in the southern part of the country. They serve their own wonderful products at Taste of Life (which is connected to the small chain of Soul Vegetarian Cafés in the United States). When we ate there, their tender seitan was topped with a tasty gravy. The server shared the recipe with me, which I've interpreted below. There's not much to it, honestly, but it's quick and tasty. Serve it over grains, mashed potatoes, seitan, and tempeh. See a good use for it in Tofu and Seitan Mixed Grill (page 44).

MAKES ABOUT 1¼ CUPS

1 cup vegetable broth
2 tablespoons reduced-sodium soy sauce
2 tablespoons cornstarch
¼ teaspoon dried basil
2 tablespoons nutritional yeast

PER ¼ CUP
Calories: 28
Total fat: 0 g
Protein: 2 g
Carbohydrates: 5 g
Fiber: 1 g
Sodium: 285 mg

1   Heat the broth and soy sauce in a small saucepan.

2   In a small container, combine the cornstarch with just enough water to dissolve. When the broth and soy sauce mixture is at a steady simmer, slowly add the cornstarch, whisking constantly until the liquid is thickened.

3   Remove from the heat and whisk in the basil and yeast. Use at once over seitan, tofu, or mashed potatoes.

Spinach-Miso Pesto

Spread on crostini or bruschetta, this makes a nice appetizer to precede a pasta dinner. It can also be spread on potatoes, tossed with pasta, or used as a condiment in wraps. I especially like it as a sauce for Very Green Veggie Pesto Pizza (page 142).

Combine all the ingredients in a food processor. Process until pureed, but with a bit of texture remaining. Use immediately; this is best soon after it's made.

MAKES ABOUT 1½ CUPS

4 to 5 ounces baby spinach
¼ cup fresh basil leaves
¼ cup fresh parsley leaves
¼ cup toasted walnuts or pine nuts
2 scallions, green parts only, optional
2 tablespoons miso, preferably mellow white
1 tablespoon lemon juice

PER ¼ CUP
Calories: 48
Total fat: 3 g
Protein: 2 g
Carbohydrates: 4 g
Fiber: 1 g
Sodium: 220 mg

Instant Roasted Red Pepper Sauce

Featured with Big Quesadillas with Black Beans, Broccoli, and Portobello Mushrooms (page 146), you can also pour this offbeat sauce over potatoes, sweet potatoes, and grains.

MAKES ABOUT 1 1/2 CUPS

3/4 cup firm silken tofu (about half of a 12.3-ounce package)

One 6-ounce jar roasted red peppers, drained

Handful of cilantro or parsley leaves

2 tablespoons lime juice

1/2 teaspoon salt

PER 1/4 CUP
Calories: 20
Total fat: 1 g
Protein: 2 g
Carbohydrates: 2 g
Fiber: 0 g
Sodium: 155 mg

Combine all the ingredients in a food processor or the container of an immersion blender. Process until smooth, then transfer to a spouted container.

Basic Vinaigrette

As a marinade and an all-purpose dressing for salads and slaws, I find this recipe indispensable. Increase the proportion of vinegar if you prefer a more pungent taste.

Combine all ingredients in a tightly lidded jar and shake thoroughly. Shake well before each use. Refrigerate whatever is not used at once; bring to room temperature before using.

MAKES ABOUT $^3/_4$ CUP

1/2 cup extra virgin olive oil
1/4 to 1/3 cup balsamic or apple cider vinegar, to taste
1 tablespoon lemon juice
1 tablespoon Dijon-style mustard
1 teaspoon agave nectar or natural granulated sugar
1 teaspoon Italian or salt-free all-purpose seasoning

PER 2-TABLESPOON SERVING
Calories: 180
Total fat: 19 g
Protein: 0 g
Carbohydrates: 3 g
Fiber: 0 g
Sodium: 65 mg

Sesame-Ginger Salad Dressing

This is a most useful dressing for me—perhaps even more so than the basic vinaigrette in the previous recipe. I love how it tastes on crisp salads, giving them an Asian accent. You can also use this on cooked Asian noodles to make an easy side dish.

MAKES ABOUT 1 CUP

1/3 cup light olive oil

2 tablespoons dark sesame oil

1/3 cup rice vinegar or white wine
  vinegar

1 tablespoon agave nectar or maple
  syrup

1 tablespoon reduced-sodium soy
  sauce

1 teaspoon grated fresh ginger, or
  more to taste

1 tablespoon sesame seeds

PER 2-TABLESPOON SERVING
Calories: 124
Total fat: 13 g
Protein: 0 g
Carbohydrates: 2 g
Fiber: 0 g
Sodium: 70 mg

Combine all ingredients in a tightly lidded jar. Shake well before each use. Refrigerate whatever is not used at once; bring to room temperature before using.

Salsa and Olive Oil Salad Dressing

This dressing can be made in no time flat and offers an offbeat alternative for jazzing up green salads.

Combine the ingredients in a cruet and shake well. If the salsa is very chunky, you may want to first whirl the ingredients in a food processor or process briefly with an immersion blender. Refrigerate whatever is not used at once; bring to room temperature before using.

MAKES ABOUT 1 CUP

2/3 cup salsa, any variety
1/3 cup extra virgin olive oil
Juice of 1/2 to 1 lemon, to taste
6 to 8 fresh basil leaves, finely chopped

PER 2-TABLESPOON SERVING
Calories: 90
Total fat: 9 g
Protein: 0 g
Carbohydrates: 1 g
Fiber: 0 g
Sodium: 130 mg

Pineapple Salsa

Easy to make and deliciously different, this lively salsa can be served with tortillas as an accompaniment or appetizer for a Southwestern-style meal. See Big Quesadillas with Refried Beans, Spinach, and Avocado (page 145), in which this is used as a topping.

MAKES ABOUT 1½ CUPS

1 cup well-drained canned crushed pineapple

1 medium tomato, finely chopped

¼ cup minced red bell pepper

1 hot chile, seeded and minced, or one 4-ounce can chopped mild green chiles

1 tablespoon lemon or lime juice

2 tablespoons minced fresh cilantro, or more to taste

PER ¼-CUP SERVING
Calories: 23
Total fat: 0 g
Protein: 0 g
Carbohydrates: 6 g
Fiber: 1 g
Sodium: 5 mg

Combine all the ingredients in a small serving container and stir together.

Apricot Chutney

A dollop of sweet-tart chutney is a nice way to dress up both spicy curried and mild grain and bean dishes.

1   Heat the oil in a saucepan. Add the onion and sauté over medium heat until golden.

2   Add the remaining ingredients and bring to a gentle simmer. Cook over low heat, covered, for 15 to 20 minutes. The consistency should be moist, but not liquidy. If excess liquid remains, uncover and cook until thickened.

3   Let cool to room temperature and serve, or store in a jar, refrigerated, until needed. Bring to room temperature to serve. Serve in small portions as a relish.

MAKES ABOUT 2 CUPS,
8 SERVINGS OR MORE

1 tablespoon olive oil or other light vegetable oil
1 large onion, finely chopped
1 medium tart apple, peeled, cored, and diced
1 heaping cup chopped dried apricots
$1/3$ cup orange juice, preferably fresh
1 teaspoon grated fresh ginger, or more to taste
Juice of $1/2$ lemon
2 tablespoons apple cider vinegar
Cayenne pepper to taste

PER $1/4$-CUP SERVING
Calories: 39
Total fat: 2 g
Protein: 0 g
Carbohydrates: 6 g
Fiber: 1 g
Sodium: 1 mg

Caramel Pudding

Chocolate- and Caramel-Drizzled Apples

Berry-Apple Skillet Crumble

Butterscotch Apples

Maple-Glazed Pineapple

Chocolatey Banana Pizza

Wine-Poached Pears with Candied Pecans

Chef Beverly Bennett's Strawberry Mousse

Our Favorite Chocolate Cake

Chocolate Chip Peanut Butter Cake

Dense and Fruity Banana Bread

Leslie's Walnut-Cinnamon Crumble Coffee Cake

Butterscotch Mousse Pie

CHAPTER NINE

Sweet Finales

This chapter was possibly the most challenging one to create for this book. Not because I have any problem inventing (or eating) desserts—but because I couldn't decide: Should this be a chapter on desserts that can be made in a few minutes, then eaten shortly thereafter, or should it be a showcase for some of my favorite, easy-to-prepare baked goods, even though they can't be eaten the minute you make them? I went back and forth on this and finally settled for the former. But then, I was saddened to think that my handful of favorite, super-easy baked goods would not see the light of print. I don't, alas, have enough of a sweet tooth to write an entire book of vegan baked goods.

And so I ultimately decided that this chapter's focus would be primarily on desserts that can be made in a few minutes and eaten shortly thereafter; but for good measure, I've also included a handful of my favorite baked goods—those that can be made in a few minutes (though baking time might be longer than thirty minutes), and eaten as soon as they're cool enough to cut. As is my preference with sweets, these recipes are filled with fruits, whole-grain flours, and other wholesome ingredients. I've always loved desserts that are simultaneously both virtuous and decadent, and most of these fit that description.

Caramel Pudding

When you crave a rich-tasting dessert that can be eaten the minute it's done, this is a fine choice. I like to serve it with sliced apples, pears, and/or Asian pears on the side. The pudding can be used as a dip for the fruits as well.

One 16-ounce tub silken tofu
1/3 cup peanut, cashew, or almond butter
1/3 cup maple syrup or agave nectar
3 tablespoons vegan caramel syrup
1 teaspoon vanilla extract
1 teaspoon butterscotch extract, optional
Cinnamon

Calories: 194
Total fat: 9 g
Protein: 9 g
Carbohydrates: 21 g
Fiber: 1 g
Sodium: 50 mg

1 Combine all the ingredients except the cinnamon in a food processor. Process until velvety smooth.

2 Taste, and step up any of the flavors you might like more of—the nut butter, sweetener, or extracts.

3 Transfer to a serving bowl or divide among individual serving bowls. Top with a sprinkling of cinnamon.

Chocolate- and Caramel-Drizzled Apples

One winter evening some time ago, our younger son said he had an idea for a dessert, and ordered us all out of the kitchen. He made the caramel sauce from scratch, but it was rather involved and made a bit of a mess (though it tasted incredible). Since this is a book dedicated to ease, I've used prepared caramel syrup in this recipe.

When I was finally allowed to peek into the kitchen, I saw that Evan had combined apples with chocolate, a combination I thought wouldn't work well. Pears and chocolate, strawberries and chocolate, yes, but apples? It turns out I was wrong. We loved this dessert, and since then have had it regularly. With prepared caramel sauce, it's a snap to make and strikes a wonderful balance of raw and cooked, healthy and decadent. It looks pretty, too. Lucky me to have such a great young dessert chef in the family!

1 Line two plates with waxed paper and divide the diced apple evenly between them.

2 Melt the chocolate chips in a heatproof bowl in the microwave or in the top of a double boiler. Drizzle over the apples.

3 Drizzle the caramel syrup over the apples, followed by a sprinkling of cinnamon. Put the plates in the refrigerator for at least 15 minutes until the chocolate has hardened.

4 TO 6 SERVINGS

4 medium crisp, sweet apples, diced (don't peel)
1/2 cup vegan chocolate chips
1/4 cup vegan caramel syrup
Cinnamon

Calories: 186
Total fat: 4.5 g
Protein: 5 g
Carbohydrates: 39 g
Fiber: 5 g
Sodium: 5 mg

Berry-Apple Skillet Crumble

Berries and apples are my favorite fruit combination in crumbles and cobblers. I try to have blueberries and cranberries as often as possible for their powerful antioxidant goodness. Here's a way to enjoy a sweet, delectable crumble, minus the thirty-minute baking time usually required. The twist here is that it's made on the stovetop rather than baked in the oven.

6 SERVINGS

4 large crisp, sweet apples

2 tablespoons nonhydrogenated margarine

2 cups fresh or frozen blueberries or cranberries, completely thawed

2 to 3 tablespoons maple syrup or agave nectar

1/2 teaspoon cinnamon

1 tablespoon cornstarch

1 cup muesli or granola

1 tablespoon natural granulated sugar

Vanilla frozen nondairy dessert, optional

Calories: 242
Total fat: 5 g
Protein: 2 g
Carbohydrates: 50 g
Fiber: 5 g
Sodium: 75 mg

1 Peel the apples and cut into fairly thin (about $1/4$-inch) slices

2 Heat the margarine in a medium skillet. Add the apples. Sauté, stirring frequently, until they have softened but still hold their shape, about 4 minutes.

3 Add the berries, maple syrup to taste, and cinnamon, and cook until the berries have started to burst and the apples are just tender, 3 to 4 minutes longer.

4 In a small container, combine the cornstarch with just enough cold water to dissolve smoothly. Stir it into the skillet. Cook briefly, just until the liquid in the skillet is thickened, then remove from the heat.

5 Heat a smaller skillet. Add the muesli and sugar and toast over medium heat, stirring frequently, until the mixture turns a shade darker and smells nutty, 4 to 5 minutes. Sprinkle evenly over the surface of the fruit.

6 Allow the crumble to cool in the pan for a few minutes, then serve in small bowls. If desired, top each serving with a dollop of frozen dessert.

Butterscotch Apples

I've become a huge fan of butterscotch lately; I'm not sure if it's the flavor or the scent that appeals to me most. I love the synergy between the tart apples and the mellow sauce; it's like making caramel apples in the pan.

1   Heat the margarine in a medium skillet. Add the apples. Sauté, stirring frequently, until they are tender but still hold their shape, 3 to 4 minutes, then remove from the heat.

2   Meanwhile, combine the maple syrup, cashew butter, butterscotch extract to taste, and pie spice in a small saucepan. Heat until warm, whisking often until smooth. Pour the sauce over the apples and stir gently.

3   Distribute the apples among individual serving bowls. Let cool for a few minutes. If desired, top each serving with a small dollop of yogurt and/or a few crushed walnuts.

4 TO 6 SERVINGS

1 tablespoon nonhydrogenated margarine

5 large Granny Smith apples, peeled and sliced

1/4 cup maple syrup or rice syrup

3 tablespoons cashew butter or natural peanut butter

2 to 3 teaspoons butterscotch extract

1/2 teaspoon pumpkin pie spice or ground cinnamon

Vanilla soy yogurt, optional

Toasted crushed walnuts, optional

Calories: 225
Total fat: 9 g
Protein: 2.5 g
Carbohydrates: 34 g
Fiber: 4 g
Sodium: 35 mg

Maple-Glazed Pineapple

The flavor of maple syrup marries well with pineapple, especially glazed right into the surface. If you like pineapple, you're sure to enjoy this nearly instant dessert. This is particularly appealing when made with canned organic pineapple mini-rings.

4 TO 6 SERVINGS

2 tablespoons nonhydrogenated margarine

1/4 cup maple syrup

1/4 teaspoon cinnamon, or to taste

Two 15-ounce cans pineapple chunks or slices

1/4 cup dried cranberries, cherries, or blueberries

Vanilla soy yogurt, optional

Calories: 253
Total fat: 6 g
Protein: 0 g
Carbohydrates: 52 g
Fiber: 2 g
Sodium: 5 mg

1   Heat the margarine in a medium skillet until melted, then stir in the maple syrup and cinnamon.

2   Drain the pineapple well (save the juice for a different use) and add to the skillet. Cook over medium-high heat, stirring often, until the pineapple is nicely glazed and golden, 6 to 8 minutes.

3   Stir in the dried fruit of your choice and remove from the heat. Transfer the mixture to a serving dish. Allow to cool for several minutes, then serve warm. Top each serving with a dollop of yogurt, if desired.

Chocolatey Banana Pizza

The preparation of this dessert is almost ridiculously easy, belying its showy result. Though I'd seen similar recipes in magazines for fruit pizzas, the first time I actually had this for dessert was in an Italian restaurant in Paris, presented as "Banana Pizza Chocolatino." Combining a good-quality pizza crust and chocolate chips with bananas and another fresh fruit results in a most impressive dessert. Use a neutral-flavored crust for this, unembellished with herbs, dried tomatoes, or other savory flavors. I like sourdough, as its slight bite contrasts nicely with the sweet dark chocolate.

1   Preheat the oven to 425°F.

2   Place the pizza crust on a stone or baking sheet. For ease of serving, cut into 6 or 8 wedges before placing in the oven.

3   Sprinkle the chocolate chips evenly over the crust. Bake for 12 to 15 minutes, until the crust is golden and the chocolate chips are melted; remove from the oven.

4   Arrange the fruit evenly over the surface of the pizza. Let cool for 10 minutes, then serve.

6 TO 8 SERVINGS

One 12-inch good-quality pizza crust
3/4 cup vegan dark chocolate chips
2 medium bananas, sliced
*1 cup sliced ripe peeled pear or
    strawberries*

Calories: 335
Total fat: 6 g
Protein: 12 g
Carbohydrates: 63 g
Fiber: 4 g
Sodium: 230 mg

Wine-Poached Pears with Candied Pecans

Poached pears always make a lovely dessert, but what makes this extra pleasing is the addition of glazed pecans.

4 large firm, ripe Bosc pears
1/3 cup dry red wine
2/3 cup fruit juice (apple juice or pear nectar works well)
3 tablespoons agave nectar or maple syrup
1 teaspoon vanilla extract
1/4 teaspoon ground cinnamon
Pinch of ground nutmeg
2 teaspoons nonhydrogenated margarine
1/2 cup pecan halves
1 tablespoon cornstarch

Calories: 314
Total fat: 12 g
Protein: 2.5 g
Carbohydrates: 49 g
Fiber: 5 g
Sodium: 20 mg

1   Stem the pears and cut them into quarters lengthwise. Core them (but don't peel) and divide the quarters in half again lengthwise.

2   In a skillet, combine the wine, juice, 1 1/2 tablespoons of the agave nectar, the vanilla, cinnamon, and nutmeg. Bring the mixture to a simmer. Stir in the pear slices. over and simmer gently until the pears are tender but still hold their shape, about 15 minutes, stirring occasionally.

3   Meanwhile, heat the margarine and the remaining 1 1/2 tablespoons agave nectar in a small skillet. Add the pecans and stir to coat. Cook over medium heat until the pecans are nicely glazed, 5 to 7 minutes.

4   Dissolve the cornstarch in a little water. Drizzle it into the pear mixture in the skillet, stirring constantly. Cook briefly, just until the liquid in the skillet has thickened. Remove from the heat.

5   Allow the pears to cool for several minutes, then divide among small bowls. Top each serving with a few pecan halves.

Chef Beverly Bennett's Strawberry Mousse

Beverly Bennett, also known as the Vegan Chef (veganchef.com), is a talented and creative cook. A number of her desserts are the ones most requested by my sons. When strawberries are lush and ripe, this is an easy way to create a light and healthy dessert in a flash. Please use ripe, juicy strawberries for this; it just isn't the same if they're rock-hard and barely red. Make this before dinner, and it will be ready by the time you want dessert.

1   Set aside 1 cup of the strawberries. In a food processor or blender, puree the other 2 cups of the strawberries until smooth.

2   Add the tofu, agave nectar, and extracts and process for 1 to 2 minutes or until light and creamy. Transfer the mousse to a glass bowl, cover, and chill for 30 minutes or more, until needed.

3   Slice the reserved strawberries and use them to top individual servings. If desired, top with granola or nuts as well.

Variation   Create parfaits by layering the mousse and the sliced strawberries in tumblers or parfait glasses.

6 TO 8 SERVINGS

3 cups strawberries, hulled
One 12.3-ounce package extra-firm silken tofu
$1/4$ cup agave nectar, brown rice syrup, or maple syrup
1 teaspoon almond extract
1 teaspoon vanilla extract
Granola or chopped nuts, optional

Calories: 96
Total fat: 1.5 g
Protein: 5 g
Carbohydrates: 16 g
Fiber: 2 g
Sodium: 40 mg

Our Favorite Chocolate Cake

This recipe is one of those that has been passed around from person to person, its origin unknown. I've tinkered with it, replacing margarine with oil and adding whole wheat pastry flour. I also concocted the simple frosting, which makes this moist cake totally delectable. Our extended family's favorite cake for birthdays and other special occasions, this demands just minutes of hands-on time.

MAKES ONE 9-INCH ROUND
CAKE, 8 GENEROUS OR
12 SMALLER WEDGES

Oil for the pan
$3/4$ cup whole wheat pastry flour
$3/4$ cup unbleached white flour
1 cup natural granulated sugar
3 tablespoons unsweetened cocoa
    powder
1 teaspoon baking powder
1 teaspoon baking soda
$1/2$ teaspoon salt
$1/4$ cup safflower oil
1 tablespoon apple cider vinegar
1 teaspoon vanilla extract

Frosting
$1/2$ cup vegan semisweet chocolate
    chips
1 heaping tablespoon peanut, cashew,
    or other nut butter
3 tablespoons rice milk

Calories: 235
Total fat: 7 g
Protein: 3 g
Carbohydrates: 41 g
Fiber: 2 g
Sodium: 350 mg

1   Preheat the oven to 300°F. Lightly oil a 9-inch round cake pan.

2   Combine the flours, sugar, cocoa, baking powder, baking soda, and salt in a mixing bowl. Stir until well combined.

3   Make a well in the center of the dry ingredients and pour in 1 cup warm water, the oil, vinegar, and vanilla. Stir with a wooden spoon until the dry ingredients are moistened, then beat vigorously with a whisk until the batter is smooth.

4   Pour the batter into the prepared pan. Bake for 30 minutes, just until a knife inserted into the center tests clean.

5   Let the cake stand until just warm. At this point, make the frosting. Combine all the ingredients in a small bowl and microwave for 45 seconds, then stir together until smooth. Or, combine in the top of a double boiler, heating over boiling water until the chocolate is melted. Stir together until velvety smooth.

6   Immediately spread the frosting over the top of the cake, then let stand for 30 minutes or so. Cut into wedges to serve.

Variation   If you have more time, for a festive touch, make this a raspberry layer cake. Double the recipe (for both the cake and the frosting) and bake in two separate round pans. To remove the baked cakes intact, it helps to line the pans with circles of baking parchment. Let the two cakes cool thoroughly before removing from the pans. Place one round on a plate and spread with raspberry jam. Carefully place the next round over it, then frost the top and sides. In season, garnish with fresh raspberries.

Chocolate Chip Peanut Butter Cake

This has long been a family favorite as an everyday kind of cake. A version of it is in my first book, *Vegetariana,* but here I've updated it—no more margarine, milk, or eggs, but the result is still a moist, rich, super-easy treat. I often make it when I'm asked to bring dessert to a gathering, and when I do, I double the recipe so I can leave one of the cakes at home!

MAKES 9 TO 12 SQUARES OR 8 WEDGES

Oil for the pan
1 cup whole wheat pastry flour
1 1/2 teaspoons baking powder
1/3 cup natural granulated sugar
1/2 teaspoon salt
1/2 cup applesauce
1/2 cup rice milk or soymilk
1/2 cup natural peanut butter, at room temperature
1 cup vegan semisweet chocolate chips
1/3 cup chopped peanuts, optional

BASED ON 9 SQUARES
Calories: 220
Total fat: 11 g
Protein: 9 g
Carbohydrates: 29 g
Fiber: 3 g
Sodium: 195 mg

1   Preheat the oven to 350°F. Lightly oil a 9-inch square or round cake pan.

2   Combine the flour, baking powder, sugar, and salt in a mixing bowl and stir together.

3   Combine the applesauce, rice milk, and peanut butter in another bowl and whisk together until smooth. Pour into the flour mixture and stir until fairly well blended, then whisk the mixture until smooth.

4   Stir in the chocolate chips and optional peanuts. Pour into the prepared pan. Bake for 25 to 30 minutes, until golden on top and a knife inserted into the center comes out with chocolate, but no batter.

5   Allow to cool to room temperature or just warm, then cut into squares or wedges to serve.

Dense and Fruity Banana Bread

Wholesome and seductive all at once, this dark bread can be made in a flash. It's wonderful with tea as a dessert or as a breakfast bread.

1   Preheat the oven to 350°F. Lightly oil a 9 by 5 by 3-inch loaf pan.

2   Combine the flour, baking powder, baking soda, sugar, cocoa, and nutmeg in a mixing bowl and stir together.

3   Make a well in the center of the flour mixture and add the bananas, applesauce, oil, and enough rice milk to make a smooth, slightly stiff batter. Stir until thoroughly mixed, then stir in the dates and optional walnuts.

4   Pour the batter into the prepared pan. Bake for 40 to 45 minutes, or until the top is firm and a knife inserted into the center tests clean. When cool enough to handle, carefully remove the bread from the pan, place it on a rack or platter, and allow it to cool until just warm before slicing.

Oil for the pan
2 cups whole wheat pastry flour
1 1/2 teaspoons baking powder
1 teaspoon baking soda
1/3 cup natural granulated sugar
3 tablespoons unsweetened cocoa powder
Pinch of ground nutmeg
2 medium very ripe bananas, well mashed
1/2 cup applesauce or apple butter
2 tablespoons safflower oil
1/3 cup rice milk or soymilk, or as needed
3/4 cup finely chopped dates or dried apricots
1/3 cup finely chopped walnuts, optional

Calories: 145
Total fat: 3 g
Protein: 4 g
Carbohydrates: 30 g
Fiber: 3 g
Sodium: 0 mg

Leslie's Walnut-Cinnamon Crumble Coffee Cake

I love a good coffee cake to serve as a snack or for breakfast, and when I needed a vegan version, this recipe is the one I turned to. My friend Leslie Cerier is an organic caterer and the author of *Going Wild in the Kitchen.*

MAKES ONE 9-INCH CAKE OR
ABOUT 12 SERVINGS

2 cups whole wheat pastry flour
1 tablespoon baking powder
1¼ teaspoons cinnamon, or more to taste
¼ teaspoon salt
⅓ cup safflower oil
⅓ cup maple syrup
1 cup apple juice

Walnut crumble topping
½ cup walnuts
1 teaspoon cinnamon, or more to taste
¼ teaspoon vanilla extract, or more to taste

Calories: 170
Total fat: 9 g
Protein: 3 g
Carbohydrates: 21 g
Fiber: 2 g
Sodium: 140 mg

1   Preheat the oven to 350°F. Lightly oil a 9-inch square or round baking pan or a 9 by 5 by 3-inch loaf pan.

2   Combine the flour, baking powder, cinnamon, and salt in a large mixing bowl and stir together.

3   Make a well in the center and pour in the oil, syrup, and apple juice. Stir until completely mixed. Add a little more cinnamon if you'd like a more pronounced scent and flavor.

4   Process the walnuts in a food processor until finely ground. Combine them in a small bowl with the cinnamon and vanilla and stir together. Taste, and add more cinnamon and/or vanilla if you'd like.

5   Pour the batter into the prepared pan. Top with the walnut mixture.

6   Bake in the shallow pan for 30 minutes or the loaf pan for 40 minutes, or until a knife inserted in the center tests clean. Cool until just warm, then cut into squares, wedges, or slices to serve.

Butterscotch Mousse Pie

As I mentioned in Butterscotch Apples (page 231), I adore this seductive extract. If you do too, the scent of the pie as it bakes and cools will drive you mad. And I can almost guarantee that the rich flavor won't disappoint. You can find good-quality graham cracker crusts in natural foods stores or the natural foods section of supermarkets.

1   Preheat the oven to 350°F.

2   Combine the tofu, cashew butter, rice syrup, butterscotch, and vanilla in a food processor and process until creamy and completely smooth. Pour the mixture into the crust.

3   Combine the chocolate chips and rice milk in a small saucepan and heat gently. Whisk together until smooth. Or, combine the chocolate chips and rice milk in a small bowl, heat in a microwave for about 45 seconds or until melted, then whisk together.

4   Drizzle the melted chocolate over the top of the pie. Using a spoon, gently create swirl patterns.

5   Bake for 40 to 45 minutes, or until the pie feels set in the center. Cool completely, then serve. If time allows, chill before serving.

MAKES ONE 9-INCH PIE,
6 TO 8 SERVINGS

One 16-ounce tub silken tofu
$1/3$ cup cashew butter
$1/3$ cup brown rice syrup or maple syrup
2 teaspoons butterscotch extract
1 teaspoon vanilla extract
One 9-inch vegan chocolate graham cracker crust
2 tablespoons chocolate chips
2 tablespoons rice milk

Calories: 392
Total fat: 20 g
Protein: 10 g
Carbohydrates: 46 g
Fiber: 1 g
Sodium: 260 mg

index

242

About the Author

Nava Atlas is the author and illustrator of many popular vegetarian cookbooks, including *The Vegetarian Family Cookbook, The Vegetarian 5-Ingredient Gourmet,* and *Vegetarian Soups for All Seasons.* Her award-winning "In a Vegetarian Kitchen" (vegkitchen.com) is one of the most widely visited vegetarian sites on the Web. Nava has written about and illustrated other subjects as well, and is an active fine artist (navaatlas.com). She lives in the Hudson Valley region of New York State with her husband, two sons, and cat—all vegans.